LETTER
TO MY
NQT SELF

Edited by Abby Bayford

Foreword by
Professor Sam Twiselton

First Published 2021

by John Catt Educational Ltd,
15 Riduna Park, Station Road,
Melton, Woodbridge IP12 1QT

Tel: +44 (0) 1394 389850
Email: enquiries@johncatt.com
Website: www.johncatt.com

ISBN: 978 1 913622 50 3

Set and designed by John Catt Educational Limited

This book is dedicated to all the early career and newly qualified teachers (NQTs) joining our wonderful sector. You are never alone.

Abby x

As chief executive of the Chartered College of Teaching, I am delighted to welcome you to our brilliant profession. Teaching will never be an easy role but it will be endlessly interesting and demanding and seldom boring. It will be rare for you to feel you have 'finished' your work at the end of a typical day, week or half term. Teaching may feel like an impossible job, and yet the rewards from this role are irresistible. You will need to measure your success differently – not by tasks achieved, but through noting the insights gained by your pupils as they grow in confidence and skill. I wish you every success and trust that, as you read this book, enjoying the reflections of your colleagues, you will recognise the warmth and privilege of belonging to our teaching community. Thank you for joining us.

Dame Alison Peacock
CEO The Chartered College of Teaching

Contents

The Academy Transformation Trust will be donating their royalties to Education Support.

About Education Support

Education Support is the national charity supporting the mental health and wellbeing of everyone working in education.

Our free and confidential helpline is open 24/7 and staffed by qualified counsellors. It is available to anyone who works in the education sector, or who did in the past. In 2020 our helpline supported almost 10,000 teachers and education staff who needed to talk. Call us on 08000 562 561. We'll listen.

Our financial grants service provides emergency, short-term help for teachers and education staff who are in financial crisis. Since 2016 we have paid £1.3 million in grants to over 1500 people working in education.

Find out more at www.educationsupport.org.uk/helping-you/apply-grant

Foreword

This delightful collection of letters is a must read not only for new teachers but also for anyone who cares about our wonderful teaching workforce. The very simple but powerful format of experienced teachers and leaders telling their younger selves what they wish they had known at the time provides so much wisdom in such an accessible form.

The advice given is varied and wide ranging and is testament to the passionate, caring, and humble people who make up our profession. From hilarious anecdotes about elaborate lessons going spectacularly wrong to moving memories of despair and self-doubt, these letters illuminate one of the most powerful truths: teaching is an intensely human endeavour. Education is not just about connecting knowledge and skills, learning and learners. It is about people and their emotions – their identity, their moral purpose, their reason for getting out of bed in the morning.

People who work in education are motivated by the sense they are doing something important, that matters, that makes a difference. This is because we all know that, ultimately, education in all its forms has the power to transform lives, open gateways, change individuals, the communities they live in, society – the world. Without education, we would not have any of the other things upon which our civilised lives depend. COVID times have shown us more clearly than ever the importance of this. This means we need to look after our teachers – all of them – but we need to give special and focused attention to our new teachers. They not only represent the future of the profession but can also play a central role in reformulating what happens now. The importance of this shines through in every sentence of every letter in this book.

The beauty of this collection is that it not only contains extremely sound practical advice, brilliantly humble and hilarious admissions of mistakes but also takes you to the heart of what makes teaching and teachers great.

Professor Sam Twiselton

A poem to my NQT self

If I could talk to myself as an NQT,
I'd look at education and the world so differently,
I'd tell myself 'Go for it, be bold, be brave,
Enjoy your time with students even if they do…misbehave.'

If I could travel back 20 years into the past,
I'd tell myself, 'The stresses won't last.'
Enjoy the little things, and laugh with friends,
And colleagues, who always had an ear to lend.

If I could go back to 2001 when I first started teaching,
I'd smile at the energy I had to never stop searching.
For that inspirational idea, or that moment of WOW,
In the projects I created, which make an impact, even now.

If I could talk to myself as an NQT,
I'd say 'Don't stress, you've got this, buddy.
You'll have long days and sleepless nights,
But in the end, it'll be alright.'

Evo Hannan
Head of design and innovation
Dubai, UAE

Behaviour and boundaries

Dear Lizzie,

You're just starting your NQT year. You're feeling nervous, excited, anxious and questioning all of your life choices that led to this moment. This is completely normal. For a while, you'll think you got it all wrong. At times you'll wonder why you chose this career path. But I promise you, you will be so glad that you did!

Behaviour management is probably the biggest worry every NQT has. But remember, this is a continuation of your training year; harness what you have already seen, read, done, and reflected on. You should also remind yourself that everybody has a different style, and what works for one person might not work for another.

There will be times when you are in awe of how your 6 foot 2 'wouldn't want to meet down a dark alley, built like a brick outhouse' SLT colleague walks in and the class assumes silence. In time you'll realise that it isn't his height, his personality, his bellowing voice that commands respect; it's the fact that he has taken time to get to know those students, and they respect him for it. It was the fact that he has clear boundaries that are easily understood and relentlessly enforced.

Every behaviour we encounter from a child is them trying to express an emotion. They may not be expressing things in a way that we can allow, but the feeling that is leading to the behaviour is no less valid than our frustration that they're ruining the beautiful lesson we had planned! Each situation is different, but taking the time to try to understand that behaviour or have a conversation with that child will be time well spent.

Going into this year, remember that behaviour management is all about relationships and consistency. Start the year being clear with your high expectations and your boundaries, and use those to positively build relationships. You are the boss in that classroom, and if you feel that slipping, just breathe, count to ten, and refocus so you can always deal with things calmly. Sometimes you will have to make decisions that the students don't like, and that's okay. You don't need to be their friend, but building a respectful, positive rapport with your students will really help with pre-empting and dealing with behavioural issues.

Also, Lizzie, remember that you are not alone in this. There are so many people who want to help you. Nobody wants to see you fail! Your mentor is a source of unending support. The staffroom is a fantastic place where teachers go to share ideas, reflect, vent or even just fuel up before the next lesson; it's a spectacular place to be! It will feel very easy, and like you're being a conscientious teacher, to stay in your classroom at lunchtime and catch up, but trust me: the students you teach, especially those for whom behaviour might be an issue, would much rather you were chatting to your colleague, sharing ideas on how to help them, or even just getting the last lesson out of your system before you teach them. Talk to people. You cannot do this without the help and support of others. Everybody feels the same way so they might be really grateful that you struck up that conversation too.

At the beginning of the year, you're worried about a lot of things. And that's okay. I'll level with you – there will be points this year where you'll think you want to quit. But you won't do it. Because no matter how tough it gets, you know that the students you're teaching deserve a teacher who is as dedicated and hard-working, and who cares as much as you. You'll realise that every trial, every challenge, every difficult moment is worth it because you do it for your students who are amazing, and interesting, and incredible! In a few years' time, you'll look at what your career, and life, has become and realise that you wouldn't want to do anything else.

From Lizzie

Lizzie Poole
Teacher of MFL
The Queen Elizabeth Academy

Better a witty fool

Dear Amy,

As you start your NQT year, you are working harder than ever before, learning your craft and developing who you want to be as a teacher. Even though it's often hard (harder than you ever could have imagined!), you love what you do. You spend hours designing lessons and talking about how you will teach things with your NQT friends. You scour the internet for lesson resources, card sorts and starting points for your own planning. Whilst I would never take away from you your ideas and enthusiasm when it comes to delivering your lessons (the laminator you will ask for for Christmas in your NQT year will be very handy indeed in the coming months!), there is one thing you are not focusing enough on: what you will teach. In other words, your subject knowledge.

Of course, your own path through GCSEs, A levels, undergraduate degree and PGCE study will give you a good, broad knowledge. You can write about books – but how well can you really teach them?

It will take you a little while (probably too long) to realise that being able to deliver interesting lessons really isn't about the resourcing, PowerPoints and how many pieces of laminated card you are able to produce. What will make your lessons powerful in the future is, put simply, your subject knowledge.

'Better a witty fool,' wrote Shakespeare, 'than a foolish wit,' and if you take that to heart now you will soon become a better practitioner.

Of course, you will not know everything – you never will. And nor should you. One of the many joys you will find in teaching is in evolving your practice, learning and relearning texts and expanding your interpretations so that you can truly share in the joy of the literature you study with your classes – and the sooner you realise this, the better a teacher you will be!

Don't be afraid to ask questions of your colleagues: you work in a fantastic department full of experienced teachers who will be only too happy to help you develop your knowledge. They won't think you're silly for not knowing something. Read around your subject – find the best that has been thought and said about the texts you are teaching and devour it, voraciously. Best of all though: join Twitter. The subject knowledge conversations you will read and take part in will shape your teaching most of all.

There's strength in numbers: lean on the knowledge of others to enhance your own, and enjoy the depth with which you will be able to teach your subject as a result. You're going to have the best time.

From Amy

Amy Staniforth
Assistant principal
Iceni Academy

Bring yourself to the classroom

A little bit about my journey into teaching. It was a second career for me. After seven years in marketing and sales I decided to pursue a career that I believe to be one of the most meaningful careers in the world. Although my time in the corporate world gave me plenty of skills that I could use in education (and certainly plenty of anecdotes for the business studies classroom), it also meant I had to unlearn a lot of the things I had learnt in the corporate world.

* * *

Dear Roma,

It's a big jump, there is no doubt about it. You've given up a secure career to pursue something which you believe is more meaningful. You will doubt that decision, but trust yourself. You are about to embark on the most exhilarating journey and, although you will spend days worried beyond belief about young people, you will also laugh from the pit of your stomach more often than you can imagine with the joy of being in the classroom.

I know the image of teachers in films such as Dead Poets Society is inspiring but you do not have to put on a show. Teaching is about bringing yourself to the classroom. The part of you that shows you care but will not have anyone push their luck. Kids can spot a fake a mile away. Bring your authentic self to the classroom each day, share your passion for the subject, aspire to grow and that is enough.

You do not need to mimic those who you deem successful around you. Even if the head praises them. Kids will adapt to the style of teaching you feel most comfortable with. You will notice they will respond to the teacher that jumps around the class with joy and also lean in to listen to the teacher who gives quiet, purposeful instruction. Just like you don't want to watch the same movie over and over again, the students don't want all their teachers to be the same.

This is not a performance. You are here to pass on your passion for learning, to apply it to the wonders of the world and to ask questions, some of which there are no answers to. Do it in the best way you can. Be sincere. See the students for their potential and you will win their trust – and they will win yours.

From Roma

Roma Dhameja
Vice Principal
Lionheart Academies Trust

Confidence, confidence, confidence

Finally, I'm a teacher. Three years of hard work and here I am, standing in awe at a blank canvas which is MY very own classroom. The daunting realisation that now is the time to put theory into practice. But I'm prepared, of course I am. I've sat in lecture after lecture; I've read books, journals and articles; I've completed three placements and was graded 'outstanding' at the end of it. Get in! The confident start I'd dreamt of.

Fast forward four months. It's January, 6 p.m. and I'm the only teacher left. I'm sat, still staring at the page of 'development points' I was given following my observation yesterday. The caretaker is stood patiently outside my door waiting for me to leave, just as he was the night before. 'I can't leave,' I thought, panicking. I scooped up the pile of papers that still needed laminating ready for the next day. But it's fine because I've already planned my five differentiated activities (as told to) and updated my display boards for the third time this term, so there's not much more to do. It's now 11 p.m.; my sheets are laminated, resources cut out and alarm set for 5.30. I'm lying in bed with the same nagging self-doubt: *What if I'm not right for the job? Why are my lessons never good enough? What do I need to do to get better? Why did no one warn me of these unrealistic expectations?*

* * *

Dear Tanya,

You are entering the most rewarding, exciting but challenging career and you should be SO excited. Your time at university has led you to this moment: you have built up a portfolio of knowledge, skills and strategies; you have observed and been observed; you have planned lessons and taught children...not too scary, eh! Your NQT year will involve all of those things too, but I am going to be honest and tell you that it will be difficult. On the difficult days, PLEASE remember: it is normal to feel worried. Please remember why you started in the first place and the excitement you felt walking into your class for the first time. But, most importantly, please be **confident** – always.

Be confident in your own ability. You are qualified, you are capable and you are STILL LEARNING. This means you will still attend training days and you will still observe your fellow colleagues. This may be overwhelming at times; sitting in awe, watching, what appears to you as effortless, perfect lessons. But please remember that they are more experienced and have had years to develop a schema of knowledge. A schema built up of successes and failures, lessons learnt and unique experiences of their own. Don't *compare* yourself to them; instead, take the good practice you observe and try it in your own class, build up your own library of knowledge and know that one day, an NQT may be watching you teach, feeling the same.

Be confident in your own development. Everybody progresses at different rates! Yes, things won't always go as planned and yes, you will be given 'development points' and constructive feedback. But please remember that you can't develop everything simultaneously; you will progress naturally, so focus on the aspects which are vital for your classroom management. Commit to a never-ending cycle of self-reflection, learn from your mistakes and don't let people put you down. It takes time to improve your practice, so please, be kind to yourself.

Be confident to take risks and divert away from the expected. We often invest our time trying to deliver lessons in the textbook way: in the way you were told to at university, or even by a more traditional teacher you know. Although they often mean well, make your own judgement: Is this approach suitable for *MY* class? Will this lesson structure have the desired impact I want it to? Does it have purpose or is it a tick-box activity? **Think: time vs impact.** Risks, by their very nature, will either pay off and be the best thing you do or simply not go to plan. But unless you try, how will you know?

Be confident to ask questions. I am finishing on what I feel is the best advice I can give. As Albert Einstein once said, 'The important thing is to not stop questioning.' It is only your first year teaching so, of course, there will be countless questions unanswered. Please don't doubt yourself in silence and feel as though you can't raise your concerns or share your views (especially if something just doesn't feel right). Undoubtedly, asking questions is the best way to learn. Just because you're now the one stood, in charge, at the front of the class – it doesn't mean you are alone.

From 'Confident Tanya' – I'm glad you won ♥

Tanya Kempson
Personal development lead
Caldmore Primary Academy

Different class

Dear Neil,

That summer was glorious. Long and hot. The last knockings of the student life that you had lived for the past few years had been squeezed out to the final second. The battle of Britpop had found in favour of Blur and here you were, arriving for your first day at work, complete with your Damon Albarn haircut and the sounds of the seminal album *Different Class* by Pulp being teased out of the cassette player in your battered blue Vauxhall Astra. You hoped Mr Jarvis Cocker was wrong when he claimed that the future you had mapped out was nothing much to shout about!

Jarvis was clearly wrong as there was no plan and the move into teaching was hardly mapped out. You had enjoyed learning immensely at school, your greyscale suburban upbringing being coloured with wonderful stories and knowledge from other worlds. But it had happened accidentally one day as you had volunteered to support a local primary school and were told that you had a natural way of engendering enthusiasm for learning in young people. You had enjoyed it too – seeing their eyes widen and fielding their questions as you inhabited and brought to life different periods and cultures. Two years later and you were sitting in the car park of a comprehensive school in Atherstone, plucking up the courage to enter the front door and become a proper teacher!

So, picture the scene. It was a hot September morning when you arrived for your first day quite early. You topped your shirt and tie with a black sweater as you still did not own a suit. Your pad and stationery was packed

23

into your rucksack. As you trundled into Queen Elizabeth School, hopes and fears crashing into the bag of nerves tethered to your stomach, your senses were filled by the chaos of floor polish and disinfectant. Heading towards humanities, you heard a voice boom, 'You, boy, where are you going?' There was an unwritten school rule that pupils were not allowed to pass by the corridor outside of the headteacher's study. In heading towards humanities, you had tramped on the forbidden corridor in a jumper reminiscent of the school uniform. You turned to see a senior leader who had interviewed you six months previously and who had now mistaken you for a lower school pupil committing the cardinal sin of traversing the headteacher's corridor. After realising his mistake, there were some nervous laughs and handshakes, but how would you recover from a start like this?

But you soon settled. You got used to the ways of the staffroom – with everyone seeming to have their own mugs and seats. You laughed heartily along with the senior leader as he regaled colleagues with the story of how you were mistaken for a pupil on your first day and, yes, you bought a suit so that it never happened again. You were taken under the wing of a colleague who appointed himself as your mentor and taught you that teachers make a difference every day. He believed in you for some unfathomable reason and told you to be a sponge soaking up every experience and seeing as much learning as possible. You built relationships with students and supported them to the hilt. In particular, you fought for your tutor group, who you adored and who you championed as a parent would. It was exhausting, but every day was exciting and different. You prided yourself on defying the cliché that your immune system would never withstand the pathogen warfare of 700 people by attending school every day in that NQT year.

In the October of your NQT year, your self-appointed mentor threw you some bibs and told you that you would be managing the year 8 football team. Your mentor stood behind you as you started to coach and form a team which started winning matches. Together, your confidence and that of the team began to build, and at the end of your NQT year, the team won the coveted Fazeley Shield. Queen Elizabeth had not won a shield for many a year and the headteacher stood proudly on the touchline, marvelling at this group of pupils who were disorganised, dishevelled and unconfident in September but who were now playing total football in the sunshine to win regional silverware. As one pupil triumphantly shouted at the shrill sounding of the final whistle, 'I can't believe we won, I have never won anything in my life.' You knew that this was a very special profession in which the rewards of transforming the lives of young people were profound and deeply felt.

On the way home from the cup triumph, you and your mentor parked the school bus to buy chips for the team as a reward. On return, with an armful of chips, you approached the bus and it started to rock with the boys' chanting your name in some form of terrace reverence. Your mentor remarked, 'It's been a good year. You make a difference every day!'

My 2020 self smiled and nodded in acknowledgement to my NQT self as I proudly trod the same steps in returning to my first school as principal in April 2020. As I now regularly remind my amazing colleagues, 'You make a difference every day.'

And, Mr Cocker, you were completely wrong!

From Neil

Neil Harding
Principal
The Queen Elizabeth Academy

Done is better than perfect!

Dear Mary,

Welcome to your first year of teaching! This will be an adventure, and, like all good adventures, there will be plenty of ups and one or two downs. Here are some things that I found helpful when I was starting out.

Get enough sleep

If you don't get enough sleep, you will feel pretty ropey pretty quickly. Aim for seven hours at least. If you're not getting that amount at the moment, start going to bed 15 minutes earlier each night, until you are getting the right amount. I have always believed that the most important thing is to be fresh and the best version of myself in front of pupils. And I can't do that if I'm shattered.

Learn your pupils' names, quickly

I think this is a really important part of establishing routines, setting expectations and, most importantly, showing respect for the young people we teach. If we don't make this effort, we are sending out a signal that the lesson plans are more important than the pupils. They are very forgiving if we forget early on, as long as we keep trying. If a pupil has a name which is unfamiliar to us, it's important to check how they would like it pronounced. Knowing pupils' names early on means that discipline is much easier: we can ask a pupil by name to get back on track – if they've gone off track, that is!

Don't aim for perfection

It's very easy to think that everyone else is doing better and is more confident and that they never make mistakes. Big reveal: everyone in education has made mistakes, and guess what, nobody died. And when we are planning, we need to remember that done is actually better than perfect.

Find a friend

It's really important to have at least one person we can talk to openly and honestly. Someone who won't judge us for when we share our mistakes and who will be pleased for us when something has gone well. In turn, try to be that friend for another colleague – it will benefit you both.

Go home early one day a week

This was one of the best pieces of advice I was given when I was an NQT. Leave school as soon as possible after the pupils one day a week. Not when there's a meeting, obvs. And no books to be taken home, no preparation, just switch off. It makes a massive difference.

Have a life outside of school

Do something completely different from school. Walk, swim, muck about. It's good for you.

Ask for help

You should have plenty of support in your first year. But don't be afraid to ask others for help and be prepared to give help when asked. When we ask someone for advice, we are actually paying them a compliment, and we shouldn't be shy of doing this.

Ask questions

Asking questions is one of the most important things we can do. Most schools have sensible feedback policies, for example, but if you are asked to do something and you are not sure how it will lead to making children's learning better, ask why it needs to be done. It is absolutely acceptable to ask questions. We can ask questions to get clarity when things might not be clear. We can ask out of simple curiosity. And we always need to ask pleasantly.

Show appreciation

If we say 'I really enjoyed teaching you this lesson' every now and then, it goes a long, long way. Pupils need to know that we enjoy our work, that even though it is tough at times, it is rewarding. The same goes for our colleagues – if someone shares a helpful idea, gets us out of a pickle or is always ready with a smile, when we let them know it makes a difference, it really does make a difference!

Use social media

If you aren't already, get on to Twitter. Find ideas, great conversations, links to research. And join in, as much or as little as you like.

Have fun and best of luck.

From Mary

Mary Myatt
Education writer and speaker

Don't sit in the wrong staffroom chair

I started teaching in 1987 – yes, I am that old. I always wanted to be a teacher – from the moment I began to torture my (six years younger than me) twin brothers with 'lessons' in my mock school room in our dining room. Gosh, those memories give a whole new contemporary perspective on the concept of home learning! I trained at the University of Exeter under Professor Ted Wragg who was, in short, an inspiration. At that time, Exeter was regarded as THE place in the UK to undertake a Post Graduate Certificate in Education. It did not disappoint – I had, truly, the time of my life. I entered our hallowed profession as prepared as I possibly could be for the daily rigours about to hit me. Or so I thought.

* * *

Dear Debbie,

So…you made it, then. Welcome to the best job in the world – truly. While not every day will be packed with *To Sir with Love* moments (look it up), you will be busy making the biggest difference to so many young lives. Never forget that.

There are so many holy grails (more truthfully, urban myths) that you will contend with:

1. **The more experienced teachers are, the better they are.** Mmm, this is most definitely true for the best in our profession – but this is not a universal truth. You know you are a very fine teacher (that feedback from those parents and students confirms this); so when

31

you are given advice from someone who apparently knows better, always respond respectfully, reflectively and courteously. It may indeed be the best advice; but it might not.

2. **Accept the professional status quo because that's just the way it is.** Speak up and speak out when you know things could and should be better. You were right to offer critique on the very pedestrian, lame NQT training and induction led by local authority officers when you did. You were polite, professional, and civil – even offering suggestions for improvements for the next NQT cohort's training and induction. You will not always know better; but sometimes you will.

3. **Some children are just beyond our help.** No, they are not. Every child wants to learn; every child wants to be praised by teachers; every child wants to know they are loved and cared for by those who teach them. Remember when you thought Tyrone would never, ever enjoy history and that he would always be a pain in your lessons? But then you discovered that he was obsessed with Nazi Germany. Okay, the initial obsession might have been a bit scary and focused on stormtrooper violence, casual racism and world domination; but, eventually, you and he connected. He became a stalwart contributor in your A level History lessons and went on to get his degree in history and politics. I wonder what he's up to now…

4. **Don't rattle staffroom 'politics'.** Sometimes, it is essential to provoke. Remember that head of department: not as good a teacher as you; paid more than you; unpopular with pupils and colleagues? When you chose to challenge such poor professionalism – by being the very best teacher, and then junior leader, you could be – some of that stardust landed on them. They then eventually looked to you for inspiration and shared professional learning. While you never became best professional friends, you did at least create a robust professional relationship which impacted positively on your pupils and colleagues.

5. **Don't smile before Christmas.** What utter drivel. You have learned it is absolutely possible to be the warmest, most loving, caring teacher while insisting upon the very highest academic and behaviour standards. Remember Juliet's comments in her card for

you when you left her school for your new role: 'I have never felt as pressured to do work as I do with you, but I've also never felt as rewarded when I do my best. I have scorn for teachers who praise my work when I know I could have made much more of an effort, and you seem to know when I could have done better.' Juliet has never forgotten you – she is proof that you could be strict with them and love them simultaneously!

6. **No profession is more important.** Really? It is obviously true that the responsibility we have for educating the nation's children is huge – carrying with it immense societal importance. It is no accident that the highest performing countries in the world are populated by the most educated citizens. However, a sense of perspective and professional humility is always important – as Albert Einstein famously said: 'Education is what remains after one has forgotten what one has learned in school.' He clearly did not have Debbie Clinton as his teacher! But seriously, if one dwells too much on the serious intent of education, it can all get a little overwhelming. Laugh, enjoy, have fun.

Take time to sit in all the chairs in the staffroom. You will find one that will fit you perfectly and one in which you will find your true teacher self. This is, I repeat, the best job in the world.

From Debbie

Debbie Clinton
CEO (former secondary history teacher)
Academy Transformation Trust

Don't smile before Christmas?

Dear David

It's nineteen ninety-something and Norwich City have not started the league well (no surprise there!).

You have made it! You are a teacher, a newly qualified teacher! Whoever said that you shouldn't work with animals and children? Well you had dreams of being a vet but soon realised your true calling was teaching. You'll never look back – until now.

Although your first job is as a teacher in a middle school specialising in science, your training as a secondary school science teacher will be put to good use in all your different roles, and eventually you'll become a primary school teacher. Who would have guessed it? Your subject knowledge will serve you well and you'll have the opportunity to support science teachers across a family of primary schools.

I know that as you start your first week you are overwhelmed with questions of doubt. 'Will I cope with the behaviour in the classroom? Do I need to be strict or can I just be myself? Do I really need to avoid smiling before Christmas?' Be reassured that there's no mould; you can have high standards of behaviour and show care and empathy for your students. In fact, your empathy and humour are things the children will love about you, so keep showing these! The relationships you build with the students you teach will serve you well in the most challenging of situations.

Then there's the seating plan. This is the first time you've had full autonomy over where the children sit! You cannot rely on the class teacher from your teaching practice to sort out the seating plan. It's up to you! A science lab is more restrictive in how you can set it up, so don't worry too much about that, but in a classroom you have many choices. Do you use rows or group tables? Just know that the rows vs groups seating arrangement debate is not binary. You will experiment with many plans in your career and my advice is to consider the class you are teaching and the type of lesson. Are you going to require the children to discuss a topic? Do you have a difficult class or individuals that need to be carefully watched? These are questions that you need to ask and then set the seats accordingly.

What specialising in science didn't prepare you for, however, is teaching PSHE. This is not your specialist subject, but your preparation will serve you well. As a primary teacher, we will often teach subjects outside of our specialism, so get to know the curriculum inside out. Read the schemes of work and enjoy reading around the topic. Be clear about what students must know and what questions you'll ask to check their understanding. Writing down important questions will serve you well.

The lesson starts, the children are in rows (as you planned), sitting reasonably quietly, but they sense your nerves and anxiety – or at least, you feel that they do. Are they going to play up? You've placed the books out ready and get the students into their seats as quickly as possible. Your preparation serves you well. But that nagging doubt is resurfacing: 'Can I control behaviour?' A sudden noise alerts you to look round. You see a boy moving around the room. What's he doing? What did they say to do during the training? What did the great Bill Rogers recommend? This is the first big test. You rack your brain to consider your next move. Tactical ignoring was mentioned, but this is not the right time to use that as the boy is causing a disturbance and the focus is on him and how you will respond.

Before you can decide the right response, you hear yourself saying these fatal words: 'Why are you up from your chair?' Oh no – have you forgotten that you should not engage the child? Have you completely forgotten the 'broken record' technique in which you simply say 'Sit down' until the child complies? Now the child has the floor. He is open to cause mischief. 'I need a ruler,' he says, but of course he has taken the longest route to get one. He is engaging with other children, making them laugh, disrupting the class. Now you say 'Sit down.'

Feel reassured that the rest of the lesson went well. You will learn a lot from that first class, and they will test you and at times frustrate you. You will make mistakes, but you will definitely improve your behaviour management skills. Remember, the most experienced teachers have honed their craft as a result of things going wrong. Be kind and remember this takes time.

To my NQT self – allow yourself to smile before Christmas as it will help and show that you are human.

From David

David Hicks
Designated safeguarding lead, science and PE lead
Great Heath Academy

Family should always come first

Dear Phillipa,

Congratulations on becoming a teacher – you've always dreamed of this. There's such a lot to prepare before term starts, so much work to do, and you don't want to let anyone down. But you should always remember to keep everything in balance – there are important things and people to consider outside the classroom too. Let me tell you a story.

It is 6 p.m. on Sunday the 14th of April 2002, three years ahead of where you are now as an NQT. You have been working hard all weekend, meticulously marking year 10 set 3's views as to why act 3, scene 5 of *Romeo and Juliet* is such a critical scene. In Friday's lesson, you explored in great detail Shakespeare's use of dramatic irony and the effect this has on the audience. You also covered the historical and social context of the play, such as the importance of family, especially in the 16th century. The huge wall of A4 red exercise books has slowly been broken down over the weekend as you conscientiously give detailed feedback to every individual student. There is more red pen than blue...a clear sign that you are a great teacher, right? In hindsight, you should have stopped there. This is the GCSE English era when written coursework constitutes 20% of students' overall grades. A time when it did not matter how much support you gave students. Your diagnostic feedback to year 10 is vital to ensuring the C/D borderline class you have been given by your head of department secures the grade students need to be able to move onto college. 'You can't let them down,' your inner voice taunts.

6 p.m. on Sunday evening: the time when you religiously visit your grandad, on the Yew Tree estate. This has been a weekly ritual since you first passed

your driving test at the tender age of 17 and the reason you did not venture far when choosing a university. Nothing could get in your way of visiting your grandad on a Sunday evening…until now. You couldn't let your year 10 students down! They need to have their first drafts of coursework back period 1 Monday morning, with clear feedback on how to improve. Five minutes later, a quick phone call to your grandad to explain you couldn't make it that Sunday evening, due to your relentless marking. He understood – of course he did. He was so proud of his only granddaughter, the first in the family to be a graduate. After four more hours of toil, you have defeated the Shakespeare marking. Every piece of coursework has detailed feedback, ready for tomorrow morning. You are shattered but it is done.

9 a.m., Monday the 15th of April 2002. Year 10s flow steadily into your classroom, ready to receive their marked pieces of coursework. You have already distributed the books and are just about to deliver some whole-class pointers when…the dreaded fire alarm rings. Typical! Forty minutes later and we are back in Rm 33 after the routine fire drill. You feel slightly frustrated that you have spent the entire weekend marking 32 pieces of coursework for a lesson that was never destined to happen but at least it is done…ready for tomorrow's lesson.

6.10 p.m.: You arrive home and phone your grandad, as you always do. Strange…no answer. Ten minutes later, the phone rings. You answer it, expecting to hear your grandad's familiar voice but instead you hear your dad's. Events happen in slow motion. 'He is gone.' No warning, no sign, no chance to say goodbye. Gone.

This continues to haunt me to this very day – the only regret I have ever had in my life. The day I prioritised work over my family.

What would I tell my NQT self?

1. Prioritise time for yourself, especially at weekends. We are not meet to work harder than our students.
2. It is your responsibility to attain a work-life balance. Learn how to organise your time in order to achieve this.
3. 'You don't live to work; you work to live.' (As my grandad used to tell me, ironically) We are in a fantastic profession but we cannot allow it to take over our lives. There is never a time when you feel you have finished. There is always more that needs to be done.

On reflection, I could have reduced the time I spent marking whilst, more importantly, providing feedback for students to increase impact by using the following three strategies (also explored in Rosenshine's 'Principles of Instruction'):

1. **Become a live marker throughout the lesson.** Whilst teaching, our default role should be a live marker. Move around the classroom as much as you can, talking to students, reading their work and addressing misconceptions in the moment. If a number of students seem to be sharing the same misconception or are struggling with the same concept, is this a signal to stop and address the whole class or, certainly, a number of students collectively to explore further? Being in constant, live feedback mode will give students immediate support and guidance but will also save you time after the lesson realising you need to teach possibly a whole lesson again. Do not assume that what you have taught is what the students have learned.

2. **Use whole-class feedback, where appropriate.** As you mark students' work, keep a plain piece of paper by the side of you to note strengths and areas for development for the whole class. This will prevent you from writing the same strengths and targets at the end of each student's work that, more than likely, they will not fully read or understand. Use the start of the next lesson to address the key points that you have discovered to move students' learning forward. Make sure you use examples of best practice as a way to motivate whilst modelling. Praise individual students but make sure the praise is credible and sincere. When addressing areas for development, avoid using individual students' names. Undermining students in front of their peers can lead to a lack of trust which will have a negative effect on relationships. There are multiple ways you can present these golden nuggets of information: direct instruction, a one-slide PowerPoint presentation or a visualiser to showcase your marking notes, to name a few. You could create a whole-class feedback template sheet which you could use regularly and print out for students. The important part after you have given students whole-class feedback is that you then give students time to act upon the guidance given. If you delay this, your whole-class feedback will lose its bite and, therefore, overall impact. Remember to use your

live marker skills once the whole class start their improvements, and seek out individual students who need additional support or challenge.

3. **Use self- and peer-assessment** Self- and peer-assessment are effective ways of ensuring your students understand the assessment criteria whilst also reducing your workload. Teaching your students what the examiners are looking for will give them a valuable insight into the overall assessment process. Share success criteria with them, discuss the mark scheme and explore examples of different graded work. Show them a WAGOLL ('what a good one looks like') so they can actually see the bigger picture and what is missing from their current work. You will be surprised how critical and astute students can be, especially with themselves. This skill is also vital for students when they are proofreading their work. Encourage students to use a different-coloured pen for when they are in examiner mode so it is easy to identify student assessment.

I wish someone would have told me these three important lessons as an NQT, or that I could have read this letter as an NQT. It is not realistic or sustainable to spend every evening, every weekend working, completing endless tasks. Keep perspective, put work into context. Family should always come first.

From Phillipa

Phillipa Harris
Principal
Pool Hayes Academy

Friends

Dear Alicia,

It's 1997 and Ross has just broken up with Rachel in *Friends*.

You chose the right career – or did it choose you? You chose the right primary Music BEd pathway; you chose the right university; you chose the right first teaching post; and you chose to focus on music teaching. How do I know you made the right choice? Because every choice we make is right; it leads us to experiences, and every experience is the teacher of all things.

Prior to your first day as a newly qualified teacher, you walked into the school during the summer holiday with your mum to 'decorate' your classroom and you were met by one of the most important people you'll ever meet in a school: the caretaker. He is an amazing gentleman and he'll do anything for his school family. There'll be many times when he wants to shut up shop and go home to his family, but he decides to give you another 30 minutes so that you can finish preparing your lessons for the next day. Caretakers in his mould need taking care of too and deserve nothing but the utmost respect. Never neglect your wider academy family beyond your teaching community; they are the fabric of your school, the glue that holds you all together.

On your first day, your mum and the caretaker helped you put up all the display pieces you'd carefully prepared at home (and double mounted of course). There was a music history timeline to display across the beam in the middle of the room; a 'Seven Elements of Music' set of homemade posters enthusiastically drawn but lacking in finesse; an 'Instruments of the Orchestra' display; and your crowning glory: a musical face using semibreves on a stave for eyes, a single quaver for the nose and a smiling mouth full of white and black piano keys. 'Welcome to the Music Room': a beautiful exhibition of your creative achievements.

1997 Alicia, the children were wowed and they loved the learning environment you so lovingly created for them. But there is no rush. A polished-to-perfection classroom is not the sum of your teaching. Be assured there is no shame in starting your career with bare display paper (even blank hessian) and filling it up as you go with children's WAGOLLs ('what a good one looks like'), working walls and anchor charts. Education has moved on in 2021 and displays have become a lot more student-centred. In the end, the history timeline will become white noise to the pupils (except for one year 8 who triumphantly found the Austrian composer Johann Fux three years later). In time, you'll learn that the true caretakers of the classroom are the children: they will emotionally connect with their classroom by curating it, with (sometimes messy) redrafts that have been lovingly created and proudly displayed by them and for them.

You will eventually move to a primary school and join a new teaching family – one that will become a family to your own family as you decide to send your two amazing children to school there. One is now at Oxford; the other has escaped GCSEs during lockdown but is set for sixth form with the ambition to be an accountant. How blessed you are, 1997 Alicia, to find a second school that is just as brilliant, happy and supportive to work at as the first. One of your colleagues is Miss Harris, who later becomes Mrs Owner and the principal where you work. Not only will she be an incredible mentor and friend but she will also be your children's first teacher.

Your daughter's pastel picture of Miss Harris reading to the class (2006)

You will watch many inspiring colleagues go on professional journeys with you; these colleagues will not only help keep the spark of enthusiasm alive and kicking but will also leave footprints on your heart, because teaching is more than just a profession. This second school matters. It affirms that all schools are families. We are one big family in the teaching profession, Alicia. Nurture these relationships. Friendships provide us with the emotional and psychological strength to deal with whatever comes our way. Take care of your colleagues, Alicia; be there for them and, as the Rembrandts sang, they'll 'be there for you'.

From Alicia

Alicia Rickards
Oak Class teacher and assistant principal
Iceni Academy Hockwold

Harvesting positivity

Dear Laura,

You will try every trick in the book when it comes to managing behaviour in your class, and as a newbie to this profession you will keep ploughing through strategy after strategy. It will take you a while to realise that the key to good behaviour management is consistency and building good relationships from that very first day, setting boundaries and clear expectations, so that behaviour management strategies needn't be used as much.

Being a teacher holds a huge responsibility and it cultivates an obsession with perfection. You spend so long creating the 'perfect' classroom, the 'perfect' environment and that 'perfect' atmosphere that the children so desperately need to work hard and have a positive day. But perfection is a trap that imprisons and burdens. You will soon realise that the time investment that matters is not the laminated classroom but the time you spend getting to know the students.

The relationships you have with the students will grow stronger because you take the time to get to know each individual. Doing this not only means that every child in your classroom knows they are deeply valued but also nurtures your behaviour management insights. Because you know the students so well, you will be able to tell when that child is displaying behaviour that indicates they are contemplating 'messing around'. You've been down this road before; you know it well. So you take a detour and praise them for sitting well *before* they make that bad decision.

Then there's the girl who is about to start enthusiastically whispering to her partner. Your teacher's intuition is telling you that when she starts looking around the classroom and moving her knees from side to side on the carpet, she has spent too long sitting on the carpet. So you praise her for sitting for so long because you know how challenging she finds it. One of the best things you can do is spot and draw attention to the positive behaviour. That child who keeps shouting out? Maybe they want to show you that they know the answer, or they have an opinion; maybe there is no deliberate act of disrupting learning. Acknowledge their desire whilst maintaining your high expectations. Tell them, 'I can see you're excited to share.'

There will be times when it feels like it's all falling apart. The students aren't behaving in the way you expect, one child 'whooped' behind your back and now the rest of the class is leaving. In these moments, you will be tempted to throw up that wall and draw battle lines between you and your class, ready to play the long game, removing break times, lunchtimes, any fun removed until the culprit is found. Sanctions are important, but they rarely have the intended impact in the moment when served emotionally. Rather than getting into emotionally loaded stand-off situations with children, try to take some time to think about behaviour strategies that could work; talk it through with colleagues and then take action when calm. Please let me tell you, six years down the line, there is a tsunami of behaviour management advice; much of it conflicting – praising one sanction, condemning another. It can sometimes be overwhelming. Things you'll try: clapping, counting backwards, time off playtimes, taking break times off individuals or even the whole class at points. All of these strategies are okay to use, and it will support your students' moral development in terms of understanding right from wrong. You don't have to back down but you do have to be kind to yourself in the process. Prioritise their learning, their time to explore and grow, and deal with any challenging behaviour behind closed doors. Privately managing poor behaviour is often more effective than public stand-offs!

Children love to explore and share different ideas. Nurture their curiosity, give them the opportunities they so desperately need to talk, share, learn, bounce ideas around and praise them for doing so! Remember, not every little 'murmur' at the back of the class is disruptive behaviour. You will learn, in time, there will be children who are reluctant to admit they don't understand their task and are quietly trying to ask their peer for help. Be aware. Be aware of those children who need to talk to visualise and learn; be aware that not every conversation between peers is about computer games; be aware that they will respect you if you respect their different ways of learning.

Please remember, Laura: spot the positives and turn your classroom into a bundle of positivity by influencing your children and harvesting a positive atmosphere. Behaviour management isn't all about managing bad behaviour; it is about building relationships with each other, seeing the positives, rewarding them quickly and leading by example.

You will be happier and so will the children whose world you have such an impact on.

To my NQT self – I am so glad you didn't give up.

From Laura

Laura Bradley
Strategic English lead and science lead
Caldmore Primary Academy

Highs and lows

Remember those people who said 'Teaching is easy!
You'll play in the sand and you'll finish at half three!'
Well how wrong they were – something they'll not admit to,
But we know the truth, Charlotte, this one's for you...

Dear Charlotte,

Remember the day you bought gel pens and paper?
And even got drawn to that fancy new stapler!
Great start to your term! But,
Always try to remember, keep them hidden away...

The staffroom! A place of great mystery and intrigue,
Number one place to be when a rant's what you need.
It's a source of great wisdom and sometimes a biscuit! But,
Always try to remember to watch what you say...

Managing behaviour – do this well and you'll soar,
But believe me when I say, some days it's a chore!
What works for one child won't work for all! But,
Always try to remember, tomorrow's a new day...

The emotions you'll feel – there'll be highs and some lows,
Just as every true teacher only too well knows!
Let me tell you it's worth it and it proves that you care! But,
Always try to remember, it'll soon be okay...

The planning, the marking, the assessment and more,
So valuable and important but on odd occasion a bore!
Never fall behind, our time is so precious! But,
Always try to remember, keep going, never walk away...

From Charlotte x

You'll learn so much and you'll come so far,
Barely recognising your NQT self, compared to who you now are!
It won't be easy and nor should it be, these are people's children – just like you and me.
But the pride that you feel when they finally 'get it' – nothing compares – trust me, I know.

Charlotte Tuck @CharlotteJTuck
North Walsall Primary Academy

How to be the Great Storyteller

I should perhaps explain that I never intended to be a teacher. My mum was an IT teacher for further education and, being a typical teenager, I wasn't going to do anything my parents did.

But after years of day jobs to supplement my writing work, 30 loomed and I wanted to do something where I was helping people. An opportunity came up at the college my mum taught at to support adults with learning difficulties, so I jumped at the chance. Eventually I began teaching, and after four years I became an IT teacher in the very classroom that my mum used to teach in. Talk about full circle!

But what did I know about teaching? I knew my subject and felt confident in it – perhaps too confident – but I had not taught anyone. Still, it turned out that my years of theatre directing, sales, dealing with customers, training staff in the pub and the plethora of different people I had met would be that guiding stone to begin...

* * *

Dear Jon,

Think about those shows you have sometimes watched that allegedly have a plot, but the more you follow them, the less they seem to have a fully planned sequence of events. As though the producers make it up year after year, leaving you constantly baffled.

There is a danger your lesson can become like this.

In your head, you know the activities you want to do; you know what you want to achieve; but does anyone else? It is important that you set out your story clearly. Where is the natural journey? What will your characters (your learners) experience? What should they learn about themselves before they leave? How will it give them the growth that every good story needs? How do you make sure some characters don't get more of the limelight than the others? If the story is clear in your head and on paper, the learners will know the journey they are taking and have travelled. It also makes those fantastic ideas stand out on the page during observations.

But then, once your story's how you want it, how do you engage your audience? How do you avoid it being that production that someone (who would rather be doing anything else) has been dragged along to?

If you think about it, the teachers you engaged with the most when you were at school were the ones who didn't talk down to you. Who were excited about their subject and didn't take themselves too seriously. The ones you desperately wanted to listen to but who in truth listened more than they spoke.

And what about that person in the pub or at a friendly meeting who knows everything? How long do you listen to them for?

Learners are similar. If someone talks for too long, they switch off if they feel it won't benefit them or that they can't contribute to discussions, or even if they feel undermined by the supposed wisdom of the speaker. The trick is not to enter as though you are the smartest person in the room – sure, you know your subject well, but each learner you meet is different, and you have as much to learn from their way of life as they do from your subject knowledge. If you listen to them, about their hopes, dreams and interests, you might find ways to teach your subject – a foreign language to them at this present time – and translate it to make sense to them and help them understand it.

Make the learners know it is okay to fail too – remember your old tutor saying that 'sorry' was a banned word. If they feel comfortable in getting something wrong, that the classroom is a place to make mistakes, then they will be braver and be able to succeed more. They will also be more likely to understand how they have succeeded so that when they leave the room, they can actually use your knowledge – especially if they know how it will help them in real life.

Best wishes

From Jon

Jon Burrows
FE tutor
Academy Transformation Trust Further Education College

In an MMMBop, it's over

Dear Shuaib,

You're driving into school with a soundtrack provided by Absolute Radio 90s, and it's time to face the facts: Hanson's irritatingly catchy 'MMMBop' is going to be stuck in your head all day. This is going to be a tough year, but you are tougher. Remember that one bad lesson does not make you a bad teacher and that reflection and reframing is key. No one masters the craft of teaching in their first year, so remain calm, stay focused on your learners, keep reflecting and always be you!

Make sure you spend as much time as you possibly can getting to know your students and colleagues. As well as being observed a handful of times, find time to observe fellow teachers and have pen to hand! You will learn from them and how they teach and interact with students. Invest time in getting to know your fellow professionals. Their insight into key educational issues will empower you to develop your own pedagogy. Focus on these relationships as they are a fountain of knowledge and wisdom which will guide you with your own planning, marking and overall effectiveness as a teacher. Read through your class profiles, assess your context, liaise with your colleagues and develop an insider tacit knowledge of your students. Getting to terms with what works and what doesn't will help you pitch lessons, develop rapports and build positive relationships with your learners. There is no one-size-fits-all approach. Remember that developing your own pedagogy will come with practice, innovation, trial and error. There is no perfect lesson in teaching, and we are always learning. Don't strive for perfection; strive for what works for your students and their progress.

You have a great NQT mentor who you should not be afraid to approach. They are always willing to listen to your concerns and offer advice, and they have your back. Never be too proud to tell them you are struggling or finding things at work or home difficult. It is their role to support you and be in your corner if you are struggling. They will celebrate your triumphs, help you with your most challenging learners and provide an ear when you need someone to talk to. Your mentor is another fountain of knowledge and wisdom and a bastion of support. Work with them, learn from them and you will prosper together.

Focus on what you can control. You can control your own input into lessons, your planning, preparation, and classroom. Schools are multilayered systems, and providing your students with a calm, consistent and safe place to learn is your role. You may not know what has happened during the day or what has happened at home, but you can focus on your own practice and creating routines for learning in your own classroom. Focus on your classroom and your students. It will help with any nerves and anxieties you have as your students need you.

Finally, Shuaib, you know there are no perfect lessons so there are no perfect students either, but again, focus on what you can control. When the behaviour of your students is not conducive to learning, reflect, use your school behaviour policy, follow up, call parents but remain consistent. Our students thrive when there is a sense of consistency and equality. Their behaviour is a reflection of how we handle it too. Do not take it personally. Reflect, follow up and remain consistent.

Finally, remember to be you and enjoy yourself as in an MMMBop, it's over!

From Shuaib

Shuaib Khan
Humanities teacher

In the name of improvement

Dear Zoe,

I know you will be nervous. Really nervous. You will be remembering how your hands shook that first time you stood in front of a class, strong-armed by your old English teacher, just to see what would happen if you stood in front of a class and taught a poem. You will be remembering that sense of light-headedness and the voice whispering that 'you know you can't do this'. But you can, and that voice will get quieter and even fall silent eventually.

Instead of the nerves, try focusing on this: remember how elated you felt when the students listened to your reading, oblivious to the tremble in your voice. Remember how they were eager to answer your questions and then began to write about the richness of the imagery in the Rossetti text. This is the feeling which will keep you centred throughout it all. This is the feeling which will help you navigate through some of the rough seas all teachers experience. This is the feeling which, quite honestly, becomes addictive.

It is already a funny position you find yourself in this year, though. You certainly never would have imagined you would be here, back at your old secondary school, a school which has been the backdrop to most of your younger life, ready to begin the whirlwind of your NQT year. Just you wait and see what happens when they become famous! Passmores Academy (yes: 'Academy' – it will make sense one day) will be big news!

Most importantly, you are about to be changed in more ways than you could ever imagine and that will be amazing.

This year you will emerge more resilient, more confident and more knowledgeable than before. You will relish the opportunities to refine your practice and work with your colleagues. You will build relationships which will make you laugh and make you cry. You will be challenged intellectually and emotionally. You will learn a lot about who you are. That will continue to happen again and again throughout your career. Being a teacher and working in education is fantastic.

But I suppose I ought to give you some specific advice to ensure you get to those amazing times more quickly.

Don't try to fit it all in at once. There is no rush, and taking time is a positive. Being a perfectionist is great, but you also need to accept your limits and know when good enough is good enough – for now. Try not to rush to the end. There isn't a race. Take it slow. Let some things rest and have a cut-off point. Reflecting can be just as important as doing. In fact, it undoubtedly means it gets done even better.

It's important at the same time to remember nobody is 'finished' yet. We are always changing and learning. Education will continue to change over the years, and you will learn so much. You will change your practice, deepen your subject knowledge, trial things that work and, quite honestly, despair over things that don't. All of it, though, is in the name of improvement, and nothing is going to be detrimental to anyone. None of us are finished yet and we all continue to learn and develop. It is one of the best things about this profession.

It's also important to remember that it is okay when things go wrong. We are human and not everything will be perfect. You work with a myriad of wonderful and complex human beings who bring so much to your day, but who can equally make even the most well-planned lesson turn on its head in an instant. Things will go wrong. Embrace it, laugh and move on when it happens.

Finally, remember to reach out to your colleagues. They are amazing and are all working towards the same goal. They might look busy, but we have so much to gain from those connections, even if we're just having a quick chat in the corridor and staffroom. You might seem to be in different boats sometimes, but you are all sailing them on the same seas. Sometimes we need to form a floating convoy to weather the worst of the storms that may come. However, if you keep your focus, ask and take the support where it is, then it will all work out so well in the end.

Enjoy the best moments, have a cry at the worst (it's cathartic and nothing to be ashamed of) and remember, you, just like everyone else, are doing your best.

See you in 23 years.

From Zoe

PS – Get on Twitter and the ed research bandwagon quickly. Trust me, it will keep you on the straight and narrow and get you to your goals much, much quicker.

Zoe Enser

Author and specialist English adviser for Kent

Just keep learning

Dear Kulvarn,

I know exactly how you are feeling, the night before your first day as the teacher of S13. 32 children in a mixed year 5 and 6 class. You are excited and looking forward to getting to know your children. The classroom looks immaculate with bright displays. The book corner looks fantastic, so make sure to thank your future wife for her artistic skills! The pencils are ready, the books are ready, the classroom is ready. All that is missing is the children.

So why are you feeling anxious, struggling to sleep? You are excited but you are also worried. Stacey is the first name on your register. Do Stacey's parents know what they are letting themselves in for? Do they realise that in year 6, their child will be taught by a complete novice? By someone who doesn't really know what they are doing? How can I possibly know what I'm doing when I've only been training for a year? I've only scratched the surface of such a complex job. I've never seen another teacher that either looks like me or behaves like me. Surely the school will realise the terrible mistake they've made and come to their senses?

The main thing you're worried about is how the children will respond to you. Will they like you? Will they listen to you? Will they respect you? You are worried about their behaviour. Well, stop worrying please, mate! What you don't realise is that the children are more worried about what you will think of them than what they'll think of you. They want you to like them, to listen to them, to respect them. They want you to be kind. They want you to be fair. Most of all, they want to build excellent relationships with you. Some of them don't like school but they want to like school – they want to learn, they want to succeed. Your first day is going to be excellent. You will feel a sense of relief and all that hard work and preparation and organisation will pay off. Your first day will be the start of an amazing and fantastic learning journey.

You will love your job, but I'm going to give you a few tips to make sure you always remain positive okay?

1. There is no such thing as the 'perfect' teacher.

Don't be too hard on yourself. You will have good days and bad days. You will make mistakes and not everything will work out in the way you expect it to. So always focus on the long term. If you keep doing your best every day, the children will make great progress over time. You will look at other teachers and think they are amazing and that you will never be as good as them. No two teachers are the same and no teacher is perfect. Just keep learning from every experience and be the best teacher that you can be. It is a fantastic job because you never stop learning and never stop improving.

2. Don't get pulled down by negativity.

You won't always agree with others and they won't always agree with you. There is a possibility that people may be negative towards you, negative towards others, negative towards the children. Remember that the only person you are in control of is yourself. If you focus on negativity, it will take precious energy away. Remember that the best part of the job is the time with the children. Take every opportunity to focus on them, get to know them and understand them. The relationships you will build with them will be central to you supporting them to learn and grow. Make sure your classroom is filled with love, laughter, fun and positivity.

3. Ask. Ask. Ask.

You don't know everything and don't need to pretend that you do. The most important thing for you to do is to trust your colleagues and make sure you ask when you don't understand something. Even if you think it is the simplest, most straightforward question, make sure you always ask. You will feel better for having done so. The more you ask questions, the more you will learn, the more you will grow and the more confident you will become. It will also enable you to build open, trusting relationships with your colleagues in your team. Take every opportunity to watch others teach and learn from them.

4. Never stop learning.

I know how much you enjoyed your PGCE. You loved the action research you participated in and the readings you had to do. You are worried that without these opportunities, you will stop learning and progressing as a teacher. Rest assured, please. You will get further opportunities and you will take them. You will drive your own learning and your career. You know that teaching is a job you will never completely crack, and you will be determined to always learn and be open to new ideas. You will remain humble and dedicated to your own professional learning. Don't be afraid to begin your master's in your NQT year. It will be fine and you will manage the workload. You know that all the learning and hard work in your first few years of teaching will be an investment in your future.

Keep calm, keep believing in yourself and keep learning. Don't worry too much about the setbacks or mistakes you make because they will also be really valuable learning opportunities.

From Kulvarn

Dr Kulvarn Atwal
Headteacher and author

North Star

Dear Lucy,

Remember the games you used to play as a child? The registers you made? The telling-off you gave your teddies for 'not working hard enough'? Remember the lives you were going to change? The world that was going to be different because of you and your teaching? The dreams of smiling faces in the classroom? This is the fuel that drove your passion to train to teach and it's so vitally important you return to this North Star periodically throughout your career, particularly in your NQT year. Let it guide you. You don't know it yet, but it will in turn navigate your mission as a senior leader at the most wonderful school.

But, it won't all be sunshine and roses. I don't tell this to frighten you; I tell you this to affirm the patience, passion and dedication required to impact on a future generation. Teaching is hard work and it can be emotional. Because you care so deeply, you will sometimes find yourself awake at night, or distracted at the supermarket, worrying that the children didn't 'get' your lesson. In these moments, it can be easy to confuse passion and determination with blame and guilt. Over time, you'll learn that there will always be children in your class who require more worked examples, additional explanations and greater scaffolding. This is part of the ongoing cycle of responsive teaching; it certainly isn't the sign of a bad teacher.

In these moments of helplessness, return to that North Star: you teach because you care. Trust in the impact you don't always see. That spark, new idea and thought planted that they'll return to in later life. Think about the different way they may now see the world because of your teaching. The kindness and humility they may show to others in their community. The love of learning or love for themselves that will change their outlook forever.

You will smile. You will laugh. You will have fun. You will make connections. You will see children grow and change and make themselves proud. You will meet colleagues along the way who will learn with and from you and help you grow. You will change.

Teaching requires passion, and maintaining that passion requires effort. You owe it to yourself and to every child you teach to keep returning to your North Star; let it guide your choices and your enthusiasm will shine through. Teaching requires all that you can give and some more. And you will love it.

From Lucy

Lucy Dawes
Vice Principal
Phoenix Academy

Not all that glitters is gold

July 2020

Pefkos, Rhodes

It's 34 degrees and even I, the most dedicated and resilient of sunbathers, have had to go for a swim to cool off. I put my feet to the sand and turn to face the shore. In the sway of the waves, my thoughts drift to the sheer magnitude of the last six months and I count my many, many blessings once again. In a rare moment of vulnerability, I am overwhelmed by how swamped and drained our profession has been and I struggle to recall the last time I had experienced such exhaustion and 'brain fog'.

Then it struck me...

* * *

Dear Amy,

There's nothing I can tell you that will be as powerful as what you'll learn from the incredible colleagues alongside you, the mistakes you'll make, the children you'll love and the beauty of hindsight once you've been around long enough to accumulate some. However, if I could give you one piece of advice as I look back at you – stood sparkly eyed at the front of your Pinterest-esque classroom with your Twinkl-worthy handmade resources still hot from the laminator, preparing to engage your beloved class in a carousel of TV-themed activities which will take them on an exciting voyage of discovery – it would be this: not all that glitters is gold.

The hours you've spent printing, laminating, trimming and displaying a plethora of posters and prompts have resulted in beautiful, glittering 'working walls'. But Amy – do they *really* work? Are they adding to the learning? Your classroom is aesthetically impressive and a real source of pride to you, but in actual fact this will serve to be nothing more than wallpaper to your children. They'll only notice it when the sunlight bounces off the laminate and blurs their vision! Think: effort and time vs impact.

The glittering spectacle of 'engaging', 'exciting' activities that your mentor so often praises you for make your lessons a real showstopper. What's more, SLT are sending others to watch you. But Amy, are the children actually *learning*? What knowledge are they taking from your lessons? Next week, will they be able to recall those facts about the Stone Age? Or will they remember only the papier mâché fun and the museum you created and ceremoniously opened in the hall? Will they be able to debate the pros and cons of evacuation during World War 2? Or will they remember only the font, background, images and animations they chose for the PowerPoint presentation they created? Will they be able to accurately explain the water cycle? Or will they remember only the fun of the card-sorting and round-robin activities and games they played? In actual fact, that 'solid' teacher who is 'never going to set the world on fire' – the one who was so appreciative of the way you welcomed them into your classroom last week after some tough SLT feedback about needing more 'excitement' in their lessons – *they* are the one your mentor should be sending you to observe! Ask to sit in on a few of their lessons and learn from them. Ask them to talk you through their planning: *What knowledge? In what order? Why those questions to those children? What came before? What will come next?* It's their cognitive science expertise and principles of instruction that your children need from you, not a circus of 'engagement'. Think: *What do they need to know? How will you make sure it sticks?* Keep the main thing the main thing; task completion is a poor proxy for learning.

Your colleagues will be one of the most valuable and rich resources in your continuous improvement, if not the most valuable one. They'll also become your allies, your confidants, your 'work mums and dads'. But Amy, remember that the glittering love and laughter emanating from the staffroom can sometimes be negativity and low expectations in disguise. 'These kids' *can*, whatever their 'issues'. The most vulnerable and deprived children need you to have the highest expectations of them. Do not water down their curriculum diet through misplaced love and ill-advised 'differentiation'. Read about fleas and the height of their jumps in a jar if you haven't already. Your five levels of this activity are glittering with football-themed appeal for 'the low-ability group' (who also happen to be pupil premium boys), but in actual fact you're putting a lid on their jar. And they know it! Think: is what you have planned for them empowering or withholding power? Knowledge is a passport to social mobility, so in your classroom this *cannot* just be the domain of the advantaged. Your decisions about what to teach have the potential to open doors and break down barriers for these children – what a difference you could make!

You are so determined to make a difference and you know the value, importance and magic of relationships. This is the best job in the world, and some of what glitters really is gold! Make sure you take the time to pick out the grains of glitter from the carpet every single day and store them. You are entering a career in which you are paid to spend your time with the most loving, creative, incredible children – what a privilege! You will meet the most inspiring colleagues who will guide and support you – listen to them and learn from them. Most of all, enjoy it. You deserve it.

From Amy

Amy Bills
Regional education director, Primary West
Academy Transformation Trust

Oberon – King of Fairies

It's 2007. I've been in school since 7 a.m. setting up. My stage is set. Propped precariously against the wall are the trees I created last weekend made of coat hangers, tissue paper and cardboard. I've wedged the football net, with leaf-shaped green tissue paper, centre stage for my audience to walk through. Despite what it might seem, this is not the morning of a play debut; it's worse. It's the morning of my first lesson observation as an NQT – my first 'real' teaching debut!

It's been quite the build-up. Yesterday, I had to beg the head of PE to lend me the football net. He initially refused because he needed it for his football lesson! My response to this was complete devastation because my observation would be a DISASTER if I didn't have a floor that emulated a magical forest. Clearly, he knew that an NQT on the edge, the day before an observation, needed to be handled with care. He relented and said I could have the net; he'd use some cones as a makeshift goal and even offered to bring the net up to my classroom after school. When he arrived, I was on my hands and knees, laminating pictures of characters. He looked like he felt sorry for me. It took me a few years before I realised why.

I decided to 'do my lesson' on an introduction to *A Midsummer Night's Dream*. I'd read somewhere that 'outstanding' lessons showed that the children knew nothing at the beginning and lots at the end, and that it's a good idea to plan an observation on introducing a new topic to show 'rapid progress'. I do hope the author of this advice has since retired.

We hadn't actually finished writing our autobiographies as a class. But my RQT friend advised me that being observed when the students spend the hour writing independently was career suicide! The autobiographies could wait. I told the class to reserve a blank page in their exercise books and we'd return to their autobiography away from the watchful eye of my observer. The class actually sighed. A boy at the front muttered under his breath, 'Well that's stupid.' I pretended not to hear him. Not because I was employing a non-confrontational behaviour management strategy, but because I didn't have a plausible comeback that would suggest this course of action was anything other than stupid. I comforted myself with the thought that we could go back to normal once this was all over.

Next, I placed a chair inside the stock cupboard in my classroom ready for Oberon, King of Fairies. My PGCE friend had recently had a hugely successful observation where she'd been told she gave the children the 'wow factor'. I'd never been told I'd given the children the wow factor. In true Boxer from *Animal Farm* fashion, I decided in that moment 'I will work harder' and get this wow factor. So, I somehow managed to persuade one of the teachers, who had a PPA when I was being observed, to hide inside my classroom cupboard dressed as Oberon, and leap out when I knocked my desk three times shouting, 'This is thy negligence. Still thou mistakest!' I often wonder why he agreed to be complicit in such lunacy. Like the PE teacher, I think he felt sorry for me. If only someone had been honest with me.

* * *

Dear Abby,

You will observe many lessons throughout your NQT year. This is exciting and overwhelming in equal measure. At times you'll sit in awe and wonder at their effortless craftsmanship. The lessons might look seamless and the students might seem as if they're just 'doing it', but this is never the case. There are huge amounts of cognitive effort that go into an effective lesson that you cannot possibly see. What lies beyond the superficial seeing is that these teachers are reflecting on how they taught this topic last time: the misconceptions that arose; the tweaks they must make; and the explanations that must be clearer than last time. They are constantly accessing a library of memories made up of successes and failures to tweak their course of action. But it takes time and multiple experiences to build this library, so be kind to yourself.

As an NQT, invest your time in asking questions to get inside teachers' thinking that will open the door into the library they have built. Conscious choices that teachers make cannot be simply *seen* by watching learning in action. Focus less on what they're doing and more on *why* they're doing it. These types of conversations will nourish your teaching insights. Highly effective teaching is the by-product of constantly trialling things, experiencing success and failure and learning from it. This process never stops for us as teachers. Schools are full of people who are generous with their thinking; they will happily explain their how and why. Every school has them. Every school needs them. Find them and learn as much as you can from them.

Whilst seeking out these teachers, you'll need to take note of the 'pedagogy formula creators' (PFCs)! You'll be able to spot them a mile off. These are often the well-meaning teachers who will tell you that your lesson will be successful if you do X, Y and Z, inadvertently prescribing a pedagogy formula. Some of their favourite phrases are 'Try a card sort' and 'Incorporate some drama to keep them engaged.' One of the most damaging behaviours of a PFC is their belief that observations are an intrusion to the ebb and flow of learning. They will encourage you to unnecessarily expedite the learning sequence to reach a more aesthetically pleasing stage of learning. Their advice will be issued with cautionary tales of disastrous lesson observations and a heads-up: 'They love to see lessons that…'

You're going to encounter these pushy pedagogy types as you progress through your teaching career. Although much of this advice may be well intended, it can be inhibiting, encouraging an obsession with the superficial and visible what of the lesson as opposed to the how and why.

As such, seek out the many teachers who will share their insights instead, and when you do encounter a PFC, peddling pedagogy to please the observer, please say: 'This is thy negligence. Still thou mistakest!'

From Abby

Abby Bayford
Director of institute
Academy Transformation Trust

Panic! At the Disco, in High Hopes

Dear Ben,

I know you think that you have perfected most areas of your practice during your trainee year. You might feel as though you have mastered the 'art of consequence', that you have sussed the knack of putting in solid routines for every class, and that there are a great breadth of activities in every lesson. However, there are so many areas of your profession that you have barely scratched the surface on, let alone come close to mastering.

Mastery is the path of dedicated effort and ongoing curiosity. You cannot expect immediate results. Time is always precious; invest it wisely. Take the time to speak to teachers from other departments about how they approach their teaching regarding both learning and developing relationships with students. There are some great cross-curricular links that you could take away from speaking to experienced teachers, in addition to observing their lessons. Be a magpie, constantly drawing on the collective wisdom of staff in your school.

Do not fall into the trap of thinking that if students struggle with 12- or 16-mark questions, fancy pedagogy and drawing pictures on storyboard template sheets are magically going to get them writing great analytical answers for these types of questions during assessments. Worked examples, lots of modelling and deliberate practice should be a staple diet in your classroom. Drip feed the appropriate techniques and skills to students who might need specific support and, in time, you will see improvement. Don't drink the Kool-Aid of 'Our kids can't do that.' It might make you feel better about your teaching, but you are lowering your expectations of them.

Remain committed to revisiting the pedagogical theories you learnt during your first year on the Teach First Leadership Development Programme. It helped you to better appreciate the reasons behind why students cannot remember the difference between Harald Hardrada and Harold Godwinson. Find out more about the forgetting curve, interleaving and speed of retrieval, as they will become especially important as you start to think about learning as a sequence over time.

Keep revisiting previous content covered, constantly making links between then and now. Revisiting prior learning is more than a 'back of the exercise book quiz' with the answers written down on a post-it note. Cement it as part of everyday learning. It is far better to spend time doing this than rushing through lessons with classes that might struggle to take on board the fact that 'manifest destiny' is more than just a lyric sung by Panic! At the Disco in 'High Hopes'. But remember, you are not solely responsible for curating learning, interleaving, or nurturing interdisciplinary links. There are many teachers and leading educationalists still grappling with these very topics. Seek advice, plan with others, reflect on what the children need now and in the future and keep responding accordingly.

Finally, appreciate and value the small wins and hold onto them tightly, particularly in those lessons when the computer completely fails and you

> **Some questions that will help us to explore teacher insights:**
>
> What were the most important learning moments in this lesson that I should be aware of?
>
> Can you help me understand how this lesson fits into what came before and what will come after?
>
> Is there anything you've done differently teaching this topic this time? Why?
>
> What options did you have available to you in teaching this lesson? Can you tell me about some of the options you dismissed and why?
>
> Can you share with me your reflections on the next steps in learning?

improvise using charades-like acting and terrible whiteboard drawings. Most importantly, do not forget the reason why you wanted to become a history teacher in the first place: to encourage young people to think deeply and enthusiastically about the past to better understand their future ambitions.

From Ben

Ben Manley
History teacher
Watford Grammar School

Patience

Dear Tom,

First of all, be reassured that your decision to return to the school where you worked prior to completing your PGCE is the right one. The relentless, full-throttle nature of teaching is going to place more importance than ever on the support network around you, and the familiarity and the existing relationships that you have at the school will benefit you hugely.

As much as it's the best decision for you to start your teaching career in a familiar setting, you need to have the courage to ask questions about what you don't know yet. This might not come naturally, and you might feel anxious, but embrace the fact that this is the start of something new; you're not supposed to know everything yet. Occasionally, people may take for granted that you worked here as a learning mentor for eight years; you may do too. But when you have questions, ask them. Specifically around the concept of assessment and data, areas that were skirted over and not such a focus during your PGCE – the year of becoming accustomed to standing in front of children and assembled adults portraying the font of all knowledge (which, by the way, you never will be). Ask questions, have conversations, state what you don't understand. The chances are, your colleagues will have been through the same.

Go and watch people. Not just teachers, but people who work with children. In your year group, in your school, in your trust and outside of it. Magpie like mad, take all the best bits from those that you watch and from social media, and before you know it, you'll be developing your own style – a melting pot of everything you see and everything you are.

Resist the urge to compare yourself too much to others because, although you may envy those people who seem to achieve silence with a single look or achieve a perfectly flowing lesson, you can't be somebody else and it's never how it seems. Success is often built on previous failure.

Celebrate every single victory, whether it's a piece of writing you can finally read, a full week of attendance from a pupil or a smile from the world's scariest parent.

Take it easy and be patient.

From Tom

Tom Reynolds
Science lead
Jubilee Academy

Plant the seed and allow it to grow

Dear Neil,

Congratulations, you did it. You have battled through your PGCE year and secured your first teaching position. You have your own classroom and a group of children eager to absorb your pearls of wisdom. The hours of planning, absence of sleep and adaptability to new challenges have made you strong. You have paid your dues and are worthy of the honour of being a full-time teacher. I know that you will skim-read your way to the questions that you desperately seek answers to. Yes, your workload becomes a lot more manageable! Yes, your work-life balance improves year on year!

You have proven that you have the intestinal fortitude to conquer the intensity of your PGCE year. Now your career really begins. As the years pass by, you will learn and continuously improve. Yes, you will adapt and adjust your practice as you grow wiser and more knowledgeable. Have no fear, do not despair; your ideology, values and ethos will live on. Your future self still looks at the faces of his pupils and sees the first human on Mars, the scientist that will cure cancer and the greatest prime minister in British history. What if one of your prestigious pupils is on the verge of making an historical breakthrough and needs to refer back to their primary education under Mr Smith? You need to be on your A game. Your next lesson could potentially inspire a child to save the world. You were right when you decided to train as a teacher, you are right now and you will continue to be right in the future: teaching is the most important job in the universe!

Although you will stay true to your core ideals, you will change. As you encounter a plethora of diverse experiences, you will become smarter and work much more efficiently. **Be proactive, not reactive.** The most skilled teachers are always ten steps ahead and in control of their own destinies. Become a better teacher by actively marking the children's books during lessons. You are giving your pupils instant feedback and addressing misconceptions early, but also obliterating your enormous marking workload. Be organised. The more experienced teachers in school will have a wealth of organisational tips and strategies. Take advantage of your NQT time by observing as many of them as possible. You will learn something from all of them. Ninety percent of solid behaviour management comes from the organisational foundations of your classroom set-up. Time wasted handing out pens, rulers and books is a catalyst for distractions and general disruption. Be prepared, be on top and take control.

Always reflect and question your logic. Do you really need to laminate something that will be on your working wall for one week? Why would you print your differentiated challenges on four separate sheets when you can print them on one? Will children become more resourceful, independent and resilient by having frequency tables drawn in their maths books for them? All children need a champion. Believe in your pupils, breed confidence, set the highest expectations and proudly watch them be exceeded. Outstanding teachers plant the seed and allow the flower to bloom.

You will make mistakes. Do not fear them. Reflect, learn and move on. You are not alone. Every successful teacher has been in your shoes at some point or another. The profession is empathetic and understanding. You will be defined by your response. However, this is not a get out of jail free card. Do not encourage your children to baste themselves in mud during forest schools (what were you thinking?). The muddy footprints on the new carpet of the main corridor will have your principal and cleaning staff baying for your blood. Also, your idea that a loud classroom is a creative classroom is outright crazy. Can you concentrate and produce your very best surrounded by a wall of noise? Unfortunately, you need to see to believe. Take comfort in knowing that your mistakes have made you wiser and stronger.

I am really excited for you. You are about to embark on a breathtaking adventure of awe and wonder. You will have the privilege of teaching a vast number of children who will shock and amaze you every day. You will grow as a practitioner and maintain the hunger and drive that you have today. As you progress up the career ladder, you will meet so many like-minded people. Many of these will radiate brilliance. Your journey is everlasting, rewarding and enjoyable. Your accomplishments will shape lives and make you eternally proud. Rest assured: becoming a teacher is the best decision that you have ever made.

From Neil

Neil Smith
Wider curriculum leader and lead practitioner
Sun Academy Bradwell

Reflective thinking –
experience into insight

Dear Sarah,

Before we start, you are embarking on a career with huge job satisfaction, in which every day is different. You have a unique opportunity to improve young people's lives and therefore communities. Remember this when you experience challenges, of which there will be many. If things were easy, you'd get bored. Some days might feel like a rollercoaster, so strap in and get ready! I'm now going to give you my top tips for your NQT year...

I recently read an education book which said that it takes 10,000 hours of deliberate practice to become an expert in something. If this is so, then during your NQT year you will be a novice. Inevitably you will want to plan and deliver lessons that are the best that they can be, which is great, but don't put pressure on yourself to do everything perfectly. Nobody is expecting this.

As you enter your NQT year, you may be thinking about behaviour management and what it will be like to have a class for the whole year. Students will test you; I can recall during my first day as a teacher, a student came to my classroom door and asked, 'Miss, do you have a student called Dwain Pipe in here?' I replied 'No,' and it took me about ten minutes to get the joke; luckily only a few students by the door had heard. I thought to myself: this is going to be fun! I have two main philosophies for behaviour management. The carrot works better than the stick and consistency is key!

Before you start in school, I would investigate the behaviour management policy. Then I would list common behaviours that students may exhibit and write down how you will deal with them. For example, if a student talks when you are talking, the first time it's a verbal warning, second time...etc. You could have a meeting with your NQT mentor discussing the list and whether they agree. This process should develop your confidence in managing behaviour, and students will respect how consistently and fairly you apply the policy. If behaviour is something you are worried about, I would recommend you do some research and talk to other teachers. But remember, books are theoretical, and the teachers you talk to will have tried, failed and tried again to get to where they are now. You need to try things out, be consistent in their application and don't give up. Expectations take time to embed.

Get to know students' names and use lots of praise and rewards. With students or groups who you perceive to be difficult, create opportunities for them to have small wins, by giving students very manageable, short tasks that they can feel a sense of success from completing. Make students feel like you are on their side and that you are rooting for them. Show them you care.

During your NQT year, I imagine that you will become quite comfortable in the classroom, but observations might be a different story. You'll be tempted to plan entertaining bells-and-whistles lessons that might result in you basically losing the plot! You will have a moment following an observation where your mentor will say 'I don't recognise that teacher in there. Please just relax and do what you normally do.' When your mentor gives you feedback, it can be lovely to hear praise, but don't take the points to improve personally. Instead, value the feedback! More important than valuing the feedback, act on it! Write down targets for improvement as a bullet-point list and keep this next to you when you are planning lessons. This will act as a useful prompt for each lesson to ensure you are focused on improving. Making changes is hard. It must be deliberate and consciously thought about in the moment. This is the only way you will make rapid progress. Eventually, the most effective aspects of your practice will become second nature.

Ten years on, you'll be a lead practitioner. What is the best piece of advice I can now give you? Be constantly reflective of your day-to-day practice.

When you have planned a lesson, imagine yourself as a student in the class who is a bit less able than the others and has a shorter attention span. Pre-empt problems that a student like this may have and think about how you can adapt the lesson to avoid these problems. Do you need clearer explanations? A worked example? More practice? Harder questions? Is there way too much content to get through in an hour? Be reflective after the lesson too. What went well? How will you improve for next time?

Finally, look after your own wellbeing! A happy, healthy version of you is going to be better for students. You need NQT friends and colleagues, time for yourself, your hobbies and friends and family. A career in teaching can be likened to a marathon, not a sprint.

Good luck!

From Sarah

Sarah Lee
Lead practitioner in science
Bristnall Hall Academy

Start with the end in mind

Dear Fizz (real name Sharifah),

Your family will be fine. They are already proud of you for becoming an NQT and achieving so much, and you will be the role model for your own children. You will be able to show them resilience and compassion and that age is not a barrier to succeeding in your life and career. You will be able to understand your children's struggles at school and they will be able to see the importance of learning and having a work-life balance. Do your best to get this right from the very start.

Give yourself some slack. You cannot be everything to everyone. Listen to the wise words of your mentors and experienced colleagues who tell you to go home and be with your family. Try to leave work at school and stop lugging boxes of books home only to lug them back to school unmarked. No one benefits, especially not you. Ensure you eat a proper lunch in the staffroom with other staff and enjoy their company instead of rearranging the classroom for the umpteenth time.

Do not beat yourself up for the mistakes you make, as through those mistakes you will learn. Even when in an observed lesson that you had planned to the hilt and everything seems to go wrong, reflect, and understand where you need to make the changes. Ask for help and ask for great advice from colleagues who have cut their teeth. You do not have to learn from just one mentor; ensure that you learn from many more.

Start with the end in mind when planning your lessons, thinking about what it is you would like the children to learn from that lesson and where that lesson fits in the scheme of learning. Learning must be built on and carefully scaffolded so that children understand why they are learning a topic, subject or skill. The letters LO (for 'lesson objective') and all its derivations (e.g. LI, WALT, WILF, WAGOLL) are not important; what is important is that you ensure that the intention for learning is clear to your children so that they can tell you what they have learnt and why that learning is important. This does not have to be written down or pasted into books.

Learn to say the name of every child you teach and make it your mission to find out more about each one of them. Greet them as if each one of them is the most important person in the world. Help them forget the bad morning or the bad night before. Learn not to judge and be the role model you need to be. The children will learn expectations from the expectations you set. Be firm and fair and teach with kindness and compassion. Set the routine for every morning: clear and consistent routines so that children know what to expect when they enter the room. Understand that the room is their safety net – it is where they will feel safe with you. When someone feels safe, they know they can trust the space, learn, make mistakes, and also make progress. Ensure fairness, monitor any of your own biases and keep your word! Trust is hard to make, and yet so easy to break.

Read as much as you can, not just for professional development but also for pleasure, as you will need to nourish your imagination and model the pleasure of reading to the children you serve and to your children at home. Cover your classroom with words, characters and language and do not be afraid to use 'big' words; have fun with them and teach your children to use them. Ensure that the class is exposed to quality stories and narratives from all cultures and sing, sing, sing together whenever it is appropriate.

There is so much I can say to you that will help you discover what a wonderful thing you are doing. You will be privileged to hold lives in your hands and lift them up to places they never thought possible. You will laugh with joy and hysteria, you will cry with happiness, exhaustion, and sadness. You will experience the whole spectrum of human emotions and you will find deep, deep joy that no one can ever give you. Remember to breathe, enjoy your family, go away to the countryside at weekends and enjoy the expansive blue sky. Look at your children (or family) and think of the person who has their trust at school...and smile.

From the person who will always have your back,

From Fizz

x x

Sharifah Lee
Acting headteacher
Dorney School

Stay curious

We go to university to learn how to be a teacher. However, there is so much we don't learn. Most of the real learning happens once we reach the classroom. It is the experiences we have with children that help us to become good teachers. Having to plan, organise and manage our own classrooms forms the experiences that really help us to hone our craft. We never stop learning as teachers; we need to understand our strengths and weaknesses and continue to grow. It is our professional obligation to the children and communities we serve. Remember, every teacher started somewhere and had to learn what they know today.

* * *

Dear Lucy,

It's September and your first day as a fully qualified teacher. You have completed the training, jumped through hoops on placements and passed assignments and now you have your own class! Thinking about how you will get through the first few weeks, let alone the first year, can be quite daunting. You will feel overwhelmed and, at times, mentally and physically drained. Nevertheless, it is one of the most rewarding careers and will be life changing for the children you teach.

You have spent all summer preparing the classroom, your new home from home. You have organised all of your new resources and you now have the most Pinterest-worthy displays in the school. Hours of laminating, cutting and sticking – who knew it could take so long? When you begin teaching and you see how much equipment is involved, you quickly realise that you need to develop a system of arranging, storing and displaying everything you need. There will also be a deluge of things you don't need, but as you progress through your career, you'll be better equipped to ward off the allure of unnecessary items. Equipment should be used to enhance the learning, and if it doesn't then it's probably not that useful. It is important to remember at this point in the year that an aesthetically pleasing classroom isn't a reflection of your teaching. The children and their learning are!

Don't be afraid to ask, whatever the question may be. Curiosity is how we remain in a cognitive state of learning. Teachers are always happy to help each other and the very best experienced teachers keep asking questions. Each staff member has a particular area of expertise that you will more than likely need at some point. The best schools succeed because of teamwork and it is important to build positive relationships, as it will make it easier to ask for support when the time comes. The most influential person you will work with is your teaching assistant. The source of so much knowledge and one of the most experienced people that you will find in the school. Delve into their expertise to enhance yours. Remember that asking doesn't show weakness; if anything, it shows enthusiasm and dedication to learning more about your role and the school.

Transitioning from a trainee to an NQT is a big step, with an increased timetable and greater responsibilities. As your role develops and grows, using your time effectively can help you cope with these added responsibilities. Planning is crucial to your success, and although this will look different for every NQT and school, there is a wealth of useful information on the internet. Be your own teacher and take time out to research the curriculum so you can prepare engaging, stimulating and challenging lessons for all children. There are endless websites full of teaching resources to save you countless hours and many sleepless nights. Find some that work for you; don't unnecessarily reinvent the wheel – take full advantage of what help is out there.

Finally, be kind to yourself! Try your best and look for the positives in each day. Realise that lessons can go wrong and things can fall apart sometimes but this is the only way we truly learn. Be strong enough to learn from those mistakes; try new approaches and seize professional development opportunities when they arise. Some days will be harder than others, but know that you make a huge difference every day to many lives.

From Lucy

Lucy Wharton @AcademyJubilee
Year 2 class teacher
Jubilee Academy Mossley

Surviving and thriving

Dear Haider,

So, you've finally qualified. I know the path ahead seems daunting, but I have some tips from the future tips to help you walk it.

Planning

The thing that will take the majority of your time during this vital year is planning. My advice is to learn whatever works for you and go with that. For you, it'll be a good idea to plan two weeks in advance of any lessons taught. This is also probably because you're a science teacher and have to request practical equipment beforehand. It always helps to be ahead. This also works to your advantage as there are times when you need to change your planned lesson sequence or spend more time on a particular topic with your students. By being ahead, you will be able to anticipate these changes and not allow them to have a major impact on your teaching.

You will be constantly told to magpie other people's resources or use lessons already taught by other teachers to save time and energy. Although this will be useful at times, remember the resources and lessons you plan are a result of how you would teach them. Directly lifting someone else's lesson without an understanding of the key principles governing its direction is like performing a scene from a play without having read it. Utilise the resources and curriculum planning of those with expertise, but invest time in planning your own lessons; this will often act as a mental rehearsal of teaching the lesson itself and will better position you to anticipate what students might find challenging.

Remember – it does get easier! A) You will become a lot more efficient with your planning; and B) Once you have planned for a lesson the first time you teach it, if you're lucky enough to teach a second class, you will already have insights you can draw on the second time round and can edit it to cater to your new class's needs.

Your pedagogy

Firstly, no two teachers are alike in their practice, so the last thing you should do is make comparisons between effectiveness. Every effective teacher would describe their teaching as evolutionary. So remember, whether it's your first year or twenty-first year of teaching, you're always a learner. One of the fantastic things about teaching is that you are always improving and refining your pedagogy; be ready to take in new ideas and learn new ways of teaching. Use lesson observations to your advantage – in my opinion, there is nothing more valuable than gaining feedback and opinions from colleagues. Remember that, and you'll always be confident that lesson observation feedback isn't a personal attack but rather an opportunity for self-development.

Lesson Observations

As an NQT, you will be observed regularly throughout your first year. Like many teachers, you will at first find lesson observations daunting and somewhat intimidating; it can be off-putting to know your whole term's progress is going to be judged on this one lesson. Not to mention, one would argue a lesson observation does not reflect the positive impact you are having on a child's life but rather how you perform in that one hour.

My advice is to, yes, prepare for a lesson observation knowing you are being observed (you're only human), but do not let this affect how you teach. There can be a strong temptation to teach what you perceive to be desirable because you've seen it executed successfully elsewhere, perhaps even by your mentor! But you know how your pupils learn better than anyone; use this in your planning rather than attempting something shiny and new. The risk of trying to do something with the intention of impressing is that it may lose its sense of direction, because it is not a lesson planned with the students in mind. Remember you would not have passed your PGCE, gained QTS and gained a job at the school if you weren't a good teacher.

When it comes to teaching, remember there are so many things that go into an 'outstanding' lesson; I'd be doing teachers with far more experience and knowledge a disservice if I was to write what is an outstanding lesson and what isn't. In my opinion, a successful lesson, which in turn will lead to a successful observation, is one that ensures your students are learning in a safe environment and are all making progress. This should be your main aim. They should know and be able to apply their knowledge and this should be evident in the lesson and in the future. Keep this firm focus front and centre when planning a lesson; this will work well for you.

Forging positive relationships with students

In your first year of teaching, you will often find yourself in positions only the 'new teacher' would face. This isn't because you are new; it's because the experience is new to you. For instance, don't be disheartened when there is that one student it seems only you are having difficulties with. It is normal to feel this way. You may observe a colleague teach that challenging student with ease, but this will often be the by-product of many failed attempts and reflects on trialled and tested methods built up over many years.

Irrespective of how long you've been teaching, there will always be times when you will have to work harder with some students than others. My advice to you is to form relationships as quickly as possible. Motivate yourself to know about the students you teach and where their strengths and weaknesses lie. Having said that, remember you are their teacher and not their friend. You are responsible for their safety and progress; if rules and boundaries need to be set, then do not be afraid to make them very clear and consistent. Students, regardless of what they might tell you, want a supportive and consistent environment where they feel safe to take risks and sometimes fail. This is an environment that is within your scope of influence. Do not underestimate the power of the culture in your classroom.

Forging positive relationships with colleagues

Teaching can be one of the loneliest professions. Surprising right? When you are first told this, you'll find it funny and wonder how this can even be possible. After all, you've joined a people-centred profession! But you quickly come to realise that there is some truth to it. Your whole day is spent with students. As such, you can go through a whole day and only have a ten-minute conversation with one of your colleagues. There will be some days when you have a jam-packed teaching day and have to rush home to your family, meaning there was absolutely no time to catch up with colleagues. This time matters; it's important catharsis. But this time won't organically worm its way into your day; you must plan to spend time with others. These interactions will sometimes contribute to the best days you'll have in your first year: the departmental breakfast, the Monday lunchtime when you shared the muffins you baked with the family the day before. These little acts of kindness and regular interactions with colleagues will pay dividends. The happier you are amongst your colleagues, the more productive you'll be with them in meetings and training days.

I must also emphasise *ALL* colleagues. There are many support staff members who will be there for you in times of need. You will have the privilege of working with technicians within your department, and your job just wouldn't be the same without them. They will provide you with ongoing support. Utilise their vast experience. There is nothing better than a cup of coffee with them at break times.

Your Mentor

Your NQT mentor is an invaluable resource in your first year of teaching. It can be easy to fall into the trap of seeing them as a judge ready to hammer their gavel. Just remember they are there to support and guide you; they have been given time capacity to help you; to contribute to your professional learning. Contextualising the mentor and mentee relationship in this way helps to ease the pressure of the aforementioned lesson observation. They will have been given the privilege of mentorship because they have a wealth of experience. Having a mentor is equally a privilege. Use the time you have with them wisely by asking lots of questions that will help uncover the rich insights that underpin their wisdom.

The mentor meetings you will gain most from are the ones where you ask questions, discuss and evaluate different approaches to situations. There will be times when your mentor will guide you to do things differently;

trust in their advice, but don't do so blindly. Do not commit to action until you have explored the theory behind the approach, understood its implementation and considered its intended impact. Theoretical conversations about teaching are not the same as putting it into action; it's important you devote the necessary time to practical application.

There will also be times when you want to experiment with your teaching and deviate slightly from the proposed plan you'd discussed. I would say it is okay to trust your instinct, as doing things differently and trying new tasks is the only way you'll learn, and that's what this year is about. However, you should always be able to confidently justify why you chose to do something in a particular way. This will allow you and your mentor to reflect more easily on your teaching and plan effectively for the future. Remember, the most effective teachers are responsive and reflective.

Your health and wellbeing

During the first half of the first year, you may feel overwhelmed with the work and be constantly trying to keep up with all your basic human needs: sleep, relationships with family and friends etc. It doesn't help when the days start shortening and you drive to work when it is dark and leave when it is dark. Don't be afraid to talk to others about how you're feeling. Seek support from whomever you feel comfortable with, whether it's a discussion with your mentor or someone senior within your school. Every school has staff who are willing to help you and most likely have been through some of the problems you may face. Be open and honest with them. You are not alone.

It's also important you make the most of your reduced timetable. In your first term of my NQT, you will use your extra PPA time to catch up on marking and recover from whatever has tired you out that day. This will be your initial coping strategy. However, in your second term, you will learn to take full advantage of this time. As tempting as it may be to make yourself a cup of coffee and scribble red through that pile of books, use this extra time effectively. What this means is, do something different that will allow you to improve your practice. You will find observing teachers from other departments very useful, especially with particular children/classes you find challenging. It will also be helpful to see the approaches that different members of staff take with students.

When you see these different approaches, remember to probe and ask why. Make it your mission to gather their teaching insights so that you can shape yours.

A final note: the most important thing is to remember that you are still in the early stages of your career. You will absolutely love teaching and will thoroughly enjoy your first year. There will be highs and lows, but that is life. Have a positive mindset, and prioritise your health over everything. It can be easy to feel like you are not doing enough as an NQT; at times, you will fall into this trap. So long as you are constantly learning and growing, you'll be fine.

From Haider

Haider Abbas
Science teacher
Bristnall Hall Academy

The bare necessities

Dear Steph,

It's the summer holiday and you have come into school to prepare your classroom for your first official year as a newly qualified teacher. You have been building up to this day for quite some time; in true teacher fashion, you have become something of a stationery addict and an interior designer overnight. Since accepting your first teaching position, no shopping experience has been, or ever will be, the same, since browsing the aisles in any given shop has turned into a quest to find something to make use of in the classroom. Your recent trip to B&Q saw you leave with some snazzy rolls of wallpaper guaranteed to offer your students a stimulating learning environment; your laminating machine from Amazon will work wonders on making sure your displays are adorned with helpful learning strategies; and your accidental stop at The Works has made you confident that pipe cleaners, masking tape and plenty of coloured card will make the most amazing lessons because the Neil Buchanans of the teaching world all suggest that the whizzier the lesson, the better.

Now whilst your classroom really will be an impressive sight to behold and your students really will enjoy that card sort you spent several hours cutting out, it's worth remembering the words of a wise bear called Baloo who once confidently sang that we should always 'look for the bare necessities ... forget about your worries and your strife.' Although Baloo might have been suggesting to Mowgli that we should be thankful for the basics we need in life to survive, the same advice can be applied to teaching. We do not need fancy resources or whizzy activities to get our students to be successful. In time, there will be three golden principles that will underpin everything you do: high expectations, adaptability and strong subject knowledge. The good thing is that as teachers we already come equipped with the former since the high expectations we frequently set ourselves allow us to act as role models for our students, enabling every single individual to reach their potential.

As happens in teaching, even the best planned lessons can be led astray since we can never quite fully prepare ourselves for the dramatic changes that sometimes occur in our students with the slightest of provocations. Who would have thought that the canteen serving curly fries on a Friday and not a Thursday, the latest elimination on *Love Island* or even just the wind blowing on the way to school would cause such chaos? And it's not just students who can throw a spanner in the works: there are many teachers who could regale you with a horror story resulting from a broken photocopier or a missing set of exercise books. Sometimes things just go wrong, which is why it is essential that as teachers we are prepared for any eventuality. Knowing your students well and keeping a cool head can pay dividends in almost any situation, but the most important thing to remember is that adapting your plans does not mean you are compromising the learning when your original strategy no longer fits. Reflecting and evaluating the success of your lessons is ultimately what will ensure you continue to offer the best for your students, regardless of the circumstances.

Ultimately, having high expectations and being able to adapt your teaching regardless of the day/season/dilemma is made that much easier when you are confident in your knowledge of the curriculum that you are teaching. We are already experts in our fields, but that doesn't mean that there isn't anything else to learn. Preparing for our lessons by thoroughly reading around a given topic is a 'bare necessity' that will not only lead to pedagogical prowess but also ensure that you continue to shape young minds even in the absence of curly fries. There is plenty of excellent CPD available to you from the people within your department and the wider teaching community in other schools and across social media. Throughout your NQT year, you will be provided with many opportunities to go and visit other colleagues' classrooms, and you will soon come to realise that the success of their lessons lies not in how many resources they can make use of or how much they can keep their students entertained but in their ability to maintain high expectations, be adaptable and deliver strong subject knowledge.

There will be times, of course, when you may come across what's known as imposter syndrome – a devilish fiend who strikes when you're tired and run down and threatens to expose, in true Sherlock Holmes style, who's hiding behind the superhero figure we present to the world each and every day. But I'll let you into a little secret – you are no imposter, and feeling this way shows just how much you were meant to be in this profession. You will make more of a difference to those young individuals sat in front of you than you will ever know – not only do you educate and inspire leaders of the future but you also support, listen, advise, nurture, protect, guide...the list goes on. It's a tall order but one you will deliver on again and again, day after day.

So welcome to the most demanding and challenging yet wonderful and rewarding career there is! Nelson Mandela claimed that 'Education is the most powerful weapon which you can use to change the world,' and change the world you will, one student at a time.

From Steph

Stephanie Badham
Curriculum leader of English
The Queen Elizabeth Academy

The cog

Dear Asha,

Welcome to your NQT year. This year is for finding your feet as a teacher, exploring the world of education and getting to know your wonderful school community.

Firstly, wholly commit to learning about your school. It is a well-oiled machine full of talented professionals of all roles, driving systems designed to deliver the very best education to their school community. Each staff member is a vital cog within a vast wheel. Each cog is imperative to the smooth functioning of the entire school. The wheel does not stop turning, so take some time to completely understand your part.

Get to know each cog. Talk to as many people as possible. Observe teachers of all subjects; build good relationships with the pastoral team and talk to the children. Proactively seek support – ask for advice on how best to implement pedagogy. Learn *about* each cog, and then learn *from* each cog.

Secondly, fully immerse yourself in the extracurricular opportunities offered by your school. Volunteer where you can. The most valuable experiences you'll have include helping out with year 6 transition, the launch of your school's wellbeing strategy and your first school trip. It is the perfect opportunity to get to know the families of the children you teach. There's nothing quite like spending the day with parents and carers raising money for local charities. The impact you can have comes alive when you get to know the wonderful community you serve.

Thirdly, we owe it to our school community to be the best professional version of ourselves. Be sure to take ownership of your own professional learning. It is not solely the termly teacher training days, although these days are super important. People development is a reflective process involving tweaking lessons for next time, pedagogical conversations with colleagues, seeking advice on how to best connect with those hard-to-reach students, the additional reading of both teaching practices and your own subject knowledge, the implementation of new strategies and networking with staff, both internal and external. Embrace every opportunity to learn and don't be hard on yourself when it doesn't come into fruition.

I saw a quote on Twitter that said 'Feedback is a gift.' Nothing rings truer than this in teaching. Always be humble enough to use it constructively, and don't take it personally.

Lastly. Enjoy yourself. Look after yourself. Don't compare yourself to others. Appreciate that you're at the very beginning of an extremely long journey. Most importantly, don't take it for granted. Teaching is a gift.

From Asha

Asha Kailey
Mathematics teacher and high potential coordinator
Bristnall Hall Academy

The glow

Dear Nicky,

So much hard work has brought you to this point – your NQT year is about to begin and you have many challenges ahead, but you will also be witness to some wonderful light-bulb moments when a student finally grasps a concept they have been grappling with. You will peer into the faces of curious learners who are desperate to know the next part of the story or who demand answers to impossible questions... and at some point this year, you will feel a glow inside when you hear one student say to another, 'That lesson was alright, wasn't it?' But it will not happen straight away! You need to establish the right climate in your classroom and forge your identity as a teacher in your own right. Only then will you be in control of what happens in your classroom and reap the rewards of what will be a tough – but incredibly fulfilling – year!

Where to start? There is so much to remember – a new routine, new students, new colleagues. My advice would be to start with learning as many names in the quickest time possible, especially the names of the students you will be teaching. This knowledge is putty in your hands – where possible, start addressing each student by name and they will soon know you mean business! Use a seating plan, avoid moving students around in the first few weeks to give yourself time to put faces to names and learn which students like their name to be shortened and which despise it! Welcome students into your classroom by name, call on individuals to contribute to the lesson and individualise praise as you travel around the classroom. (You will soon learn the students who are motivated by this and those who prefer to have it written down and not made public!) This is not just about behaviour management; this is the start of relational teaching, and an investment of time at the beginning of the relationship will pay huge dividends later on in the journey you will take these students on.

Here is my challenge to you: during a lesson, engage individually with as many of the students in front of you as you can. Show them that you truly care about the progress they are making in your classroom, that they can approach you for help and that you will support them to take risks in their learning. This will lead to your students growing in confidence and challenging themselves to step out of their comfort zone, and we all know that this is the time at which they will begin to fly! Make your classroom a place your students look forward to entering – not because the learning is safe and easy, but because the conditions are right for them to be challenged and exposed, without being fearful. Think about the teachers you remember most from school, the ones that at some point inspired you to pursue this career and spend your working life back at school. What made them great? The passion they had for their subject, the amount of knowledge you learned from them…and how much they cared about their students!

Finally, what about those hard-to-reach students? The one who very vocally asks 'Are we going to do something interesting today?' Or the student who struggles to make eye contact with you? Or the one that will only give you a one-word answer no matter how you pose the question? As hard as it may be to crack the egg, get to know them and what makes them tick. Five minutes on a Sunday evening checking the football scores, asking them about the motocross race they took part in at the weekend, or finding out more about the dance show they are working so hard towards might just give you the power to make a passing comment that changes the way a student views you: *This teacher cares about me outside of these four walls… she's taken an interest in my interests… now, let's see what she has to offer in her lesson today!*

Good luck – be resilient, ask for support when you need it and enjoy your NQT year!

Best wishes,

From Nicky xxx

Nicola Powling
People development lead and faculty leader
Mildenhall College Academy

'The important thing is to not stop questioning'
—Albert Einstein

Dear Freddie,

Cast your mind back to your teachers in school and how they seemed to master every situation. In your first year of teaching, this is all you'll be able to think about. How they were so self-assured and confident; they made it seem so effortless! Not only your own teachers, but those you observed on placement and your tutors at university too. It might be daunting to imagine doing the same in front of a class of 30 children (who expect you to deliver like a seasoned pro!) but cut yourself some slack. As well as beginning a new career, you are also stepping into a new school with new rules, routines and policies, students, colleagues, classrooms, timings of the day, schemes of learning and everything else too! You will make some mistakes along the way but rest assured, you will improve as a practitioner as a consequence. One thing that is in your control, to make your first year in teaching a success, is being as organised as possible.

As the nerves begin to mount prior to September, make sure you are prepared to ask the right questions. You can obviously glean lots of useful information from the school website and start to build up a knowledge of relevant policies and schemes. Note down any remaining niggling queries, ready for the inset days (and get a reputation for being proactive!). This is the best opportunity to ease your anxieties, and your colleagues will be there to help you. In addition to introductions, safeguarding training and pastoral meetings, there will be some invaluable faculty and PPA time. Whilst it is easy to be distracted by the exciting task of preparing your own classroom and carefully counting out piles of exercise books, don't neglect to ask which scheme of work to use, what the passwords are for resources or how to take the register!

One powerful tool utilised by experienced teachers is seating plans. Evenly distributing 30 students considering gender, personality traits, aptitude for the subject, SEND and EAL is an art form. If executed correctly, it can be hugely helpful in encouraging and maintaining a calm learning environment. Ask colleagues for their help to devise these. Take advantage of their knowledge of students as they will be able to provide context to the names and will quickly spot an unfavourable grouping.

There is such a thing as overplanning. You probably will fall foul of this at times, but try to simplify the process and have a clear idea about the objective(s) and how the students will meet them. Think of it like learning to drive: your focus is keeping the car on the road. It would be unwise to overload your brain by changing radio stations or opening the sunroof. Similarly, when in the classroom, avoid focusing on the intricacies as you will likely run out of time or lose sight of the end goal. You will still need to do your research around common mistakes and misconceptions, though, and attempt to anticipate the types of questions students will inevitably ask along the way, being ready to confidently deliver your pre-prepared answer to 'When am I ever going to use this?' However, don't worry if the best you can come up with is 'I don't actually know.' You're not expected to know everything, but make it your mission to find out for the next lesson!

I will leave you with a pertinent piece of advice: children can be unpredictable! They are unlikely to act the same on Monday morning and Friday afternoon. When a child enters your room, you do not know what has happened in their day up to that point. They might have had an argument with Mum over breakfast, missed the bus or got up late. They might still feel aggrieved after misbehaving in their last lesson. The best thing that you can do is be reliable. When teaching, make sure your explanations are solid; they will find value in prepared answers which are concise and clear. If a child enters your classroom knowing that you are also going to be approachable and fair with the rules, they are much more likely to want to work and learn with you. Having classroom routines will also build their trust and confidence in your lessons. Be consistent and you will promote consistently positive behaviour.

All the best of luck,

From Freddie

PS please avoid abbreviating cumulative frequency when teaching stats.

Freddie Hughes
Mathematics faculty leader
Mildenhall College Academy

'The only thing we have to fear is fear itself'

—Franklin D. Roosevelt

A modicum of fear passes through my mind. It's a date that I've seen in the school calendar for some time, but until now it had seemed a long way off...

I've spent the last few weeks recalling names, getting to grips with the register, remembering the copier code, being punctual for playground duty – not to mention actually fulfilling my ambition of teaching the eager faces before me. I've battened down the hatches and survived until October. In fact, I've more than survived; there have been moments of true joy. There's been glimpses of why I followed my heart and not my head and made very real sacrifices to enter this noble profession of teaching.

However, staring now at a crib sheet with names and time slots, it's suddenly become real. Instead of snatched conversations at the classroom door, I'm now going to have to talk at length to the parents of the children in my charge. Adults, not children. And I don't have a script or a lesson plan.

Parents' evening is fast approaching.

It's a chilly October afternoon and my TA has bundled the last of the children home so I can quickly rearrange some of the classroom furniture. I'm conflicted. Somewhere I read in a *Tes* article that having a table between sitting people is a physical barrier, but removing it makes me feel vulnerable. I compromise by placing it at a jaunty angle. I'm overthinking this. I put some soft meditation music on in the background and launch a montage of images captured of my new class in my first few weeks of teaching. I smile – the kids look happy. Then my laptop battery fails, the music stops and the reassuring images end abruptly. Simultaneously, there's a knock on the door and my first parents have arrived. I shake hands and stammer out a greeting. It's begun. Luckily they're charming and I can be positive about their bundles of joy and they largely reciprocate. Even meetings with parents of children where behaviour can be an issue or where we need to discuss specific needs pass off relatively well.

Then just as I'm riding high, something jars; the next appointment is with the parents of a young girl who always seems to have the correct answer but appears a little indifferent. Her parents speak of their concerns that she is not being challenged enough. They complain that she finds the work too easy and has the potential for much more, giving me examples of her tackling concepts well beyond the year 2 curriculum. They even mention that they may look to take her out of school if necessary.

It's an uneasy conversation. I'm a little mortified; how can I have missed this? Have I mistaken obedience for boredom? How did I not spot this latent talent? Will I be responsible for stunting her chances later in life? I suddenly feel like I'm wearing a hair shirt.

Although I've been dealing with the evening in ten-minute increments, I've completely lost track of time. It's 8.30 p.m. and with the rattling of keys, my NQT mentor is keen to move me along and out the door. However, she senses that there's something amiss and probes further. I condense the positive memories down to one sentence but then pour forth the shame of apparently not fulfilling this child's potential with lavish detail.

'Eight weeks, Craig. Eight weeks. Just remember that.' I see her point. I have lost sight of the fact that this is all new to me. I've set high expectations and then judged myself accordingly. But am I being fair to myself? My mentor reassures me that there is no possible way that I have caused serious harm to this girl's life chances. She also reminds me that it is possible for some parents to get carried away in the pursuit of the best for their child;

apparently when taught by other vastly more experienced practitioners, the parents have also questioned the quality of provision for their child. She tells me that sometimes their ambition for the future can lead them to some unjust conclusions. 'Knowing what you knew, did you do the best you could?' she asks me. I nod. 'Then go home and get some sleep. Besides, you've got the Halloween disco to organise tomorrow.'

The drive home affords time for cathartic reflection. Listen, empathise and consider the views of parents but don't always assume they are wholly correct or unbiased. As for parent conferences, recall the words of Franklin Roosevelt: 'The only thing we have to fear is fear itself.'

* * *

Dear Craig,

Remember, when communicating with parents, first impressions count. Be confident and assured: you may feel like a professional at the start of their career but you are a professional nonetheless. So act like one.

Don't be overbearing in your approach but be sincere. There will still be the unknown, the unexpected – the curveball thrown at you that you never saw coming. But you will develop an arsenal of tools to better cope with this. Don't take to heart any barbed comments uttered by parents.

Largely, parents want to be heard, reassured, guided; some want to be cajoled into action. Some may even want to pour their heart out to you; they need help to parent their child and you're someone they trust. Remember, for a large part of the term, you are in loco parentis, vital to their child's development.

Remember, too, that time constraints do put an artificial complexion on these discussions. They can intensify emotions; to alleviate this, don't be afraid to arrange a subsequent meeting outside of the parents' evening. There, you may even ask a colleague to sit in for reassurance.

If you can build in a buffer to your appointments then do so. Use this time to steel yourself; each child deserves for you to be at your eloquent best when speaking to their parent. Don't be afraid to ask the parent how their child feels about school. Note: school *as a whole*, not you as a teacher. Depersonalise where you can. Not all parents are going to like you as a practitioner; not all children do. It doesn't matter. It isn't a popularity contest. Don't make decisions with a thought about the quantity of gifts at the end of the year. Make decisions on what is best for the child. If parents need to know something about their child's behaviour, attitude or progress, approach subjects with care – but don't duck it. That second parents' evening in the spring will be all the harder if you do.

Acknowledge in your mind that you may not know all of the children really well yet. You simply can't. But it doesn't mean you're not interested in the child, and parents are a great source of information about those overlooked pupils. Glean from your conversations what makes these children tick. If you can recall a snippet of information about their personality and recount it to them the next day, you will be amazed at how you can build positive relationships with these young people. Remember the feeling when your teacher took a genuine interest in you?

Consider what it is like being the other side of the table; parents are very often nervous too. They may be harbouring some difficult memories about their own school life and may feel that you are tacitly judging them as parents. Any defensive behaviour could well be a result of this. Disarm this where you can and view parent conference as an opportunity to open a dialogue between you and the child's family. If you remain in one setting for any length of time, you will no doubt encounter them again, either through teaching siblings or in another year group.

Lastly, a double-edged sword. If you promise to help alleviate the concerns of a parent, follow up on this. It reflects your sincerity and integrity. Conversely, be aware of the need to manage expectations of a parent; in an attempt to alleviate any concerns they may have, you may promise the earth when you have no capacity to deliver it.

Above all, be kind to yourself this first year; the teaching profession deserves for you to succeed.

From Craig

Craig Battrick
Curriculum lead
Star Academy, Sandyford

'They are all right for me'

It's Friday and I'm gearing up for period 6 of a full teaching day as my energetic year 7 class from period 5 frantically romp around the room indiscriminately throwing Bunsen burners, mats and tripods into the wrong cupboards. I sigh. That's a job for me later. I cut my losses; so out they go. I can hear my 'challenging' KS4 class – whose interpretation of 'line up' is gathering in loud, boisterous groups – prepare to enter. Their voices are raised and some of the boys are pushing each other and pulling on each other's bags, to the resounding shouts of 'Way!' You get the picture!

Last Friday's lesson with this group can only be described as a disaster. Having never taught dissection before, I naively assumed it would interest them and maybe engage them. I was wrong. Enough kidney ended up on my ceiling (and in people's hair) to make a pie! And little if any learning took place. So after that, I sought advice from their head of year, who was really supportive. We discussed a range of strategies and, as she was free last thing on Friday, she agreed to pop in a couple of times.

So, this time it was going to be different! I had a plan! There was a new seating plan, a calming starter, a new set of expectations and lots of short carefully pitched activities to ensure that there was simply no time to misbehave. But if they still managed to give me the runaround, I had a new approach to sanctions too, and I was confident my no-nonsense strategy would work. This was it; I meant business.

They barely seemed to notice! If they did, they certainly didn't care! Nevertheless, I doggedly followed through my plan, kept the lesson flowing (albeit with escalating volume to be heard over the noise) and issued my planned sanctions. I repeatedly made it totally clear what the consequences were, yet up the sanction ladder they climbed. By the end of the lesson, half the class were on detentions *and* I'd had to remove some students too. To add insult to injury, as their head of year walked through the door, my class of screaming banshees converted meekly into angelic cherubs, only to switch back as soon as the door clicked shut behind her. Why did they not listen to me? Through gritted teeth, I still insisted they stand behind their chairs to be dismissed; it took forever, but finally I waved them off with a forced smile. A few minutes later, I entered the staffroom at the end of the day, slumped down next to an experienced colleague (who teaches the same group maths) and poured my heart out. She replied, 'They are all right for me.' It took six words to shatter my world and make me feel like a failure.

* * *

Dear Cat,

I really want to tell you: you didn't fail at all – you won! It wasn't a resounding victory, but you definitely won. The moment you won wasn't on Friday afternoon – no, it was the following week: when you made them sit the full detention time with you; when you had the calm and respectful restorative conversations with those students; when you chased the students who didn't attend; when you escalated it to the next level with the ones who missed their second chance; and when you rang home to discuss their behaviour. And do you know what else? You keep on winning, just a little bit every day.

I really want to tell you that the 'superpower' that established teachers seem to have is not really a superpower at all. It's not the way they talk, or even what they say. It's also not their job title (although sometimes that helps). Going to watch an established teacher who is renowned for 'good behaviour management' won't help at all, because you won't see any bad behaviour! Some of the teachers who have it don't understand how they got it, and some are even less helpful with comments like 'They are all right for me.' When you meet these people, let their comments wash over you. They might be good teachers, but they won't be good coaches, and if they ever move school, they'll be in for a shock!

Attainment of the 'superpower' comes from repeated interactions with students, building relationships, showing them respect and forgiving them again and again. But there are lots of things you can do to help accelerate your development of the 'superpower'. Be fair in your sanctions, and always be disappointed (but not angry) when you issue them. Celebrating positives is more important than you realise right now; for every phone call you make to discuss a negative, follow it straight up with a phone call to celebrate a positive. It will make you feel better too. But the most important thing is to always follow through with what you say – certainty (not severity) is the key!

Remember: every lesson is a new start for everyone, including you. Smile, welcome them in, and don't assume that this lesson will be like the last. Lots of things affect behaviour and a tremendous amount of it is out of your control. We all know what happens if there is a wasp in the room. Don't be disappointed if all your persistence doesn't work straight away. It takes time, but it will work! I promise. Your cape awaits you!

From Cat

Catherine Rushton
Specialist lead practitioner for science
The Nicholas Hammond Academy

Tomorrow is a new day

Dear Andy,

You're about to embark on the biggest journey of your life, one that will be full of excitement, frustration, jubilation and, if I'm honest, probably too much chocolate. You're a teacher now.

It's September 1994. You're in *your* classroom; the one that you've spent all last week arranging, rearranging and improving, making it look the way you want. I'm writing to you from what probably seems like the distant future: 2020. So much has changed in education and in the world around us. The way you are working now, with your blackboard and your chalk, is not the way I work. Your brand-new Acorn A3000 computer won't stay cutting edge forever. I remember your first classroom. I can still picture the layout: where the children sat, the optimal position for the book corner, the wonderful view over the school field. You will spend many hours in that classroom. It's where you will develop minds and teach skills that will last a lifetime. 26 years on, you will still remember those children. Some of them will still remember you.

So much has changed over the last 26 years, but much is still the same. Children are still children. They still need adult help to handle the challenges of learning and the challenges of growing up. They still rely on those adult role models to guide them on their journey through school. Your role in developing their knowledge, skills and values – be they academic, social or personal – must never be understated.

You will be lucky enough to work with some amazing teachers. You will watch them in the classroom and be envious of the way their mere presence in the room seems to ensure that children achieve. You will second guess your own teaching and think that if you only did what they are doing, you would be a better teacher. This isn't true. You are you; you are not a clone of someone else. Borrow ideas from others, by all means; try them out; see how they work for you. Build these ideas into a jigsaw of success that you can use. Never forget that these teachers became experts in their craft through constantly trying out ideas, filtering the successful idea from the one that bombed and gradually building up a toolkit of successful techniques. Learn from them, but never copy them.

As you work through your career, you will soon find that there is an ever-changing procession of fashions and fads. What you teach, and the way you teach, will change, often annually. Each year, there will be something that will be announced as the tool to fix everything; a new strategy, an improved technique or a revolutionary philosophy that will set the world of education alight. You will probably leap at every one of these because you want to be the best teacher you can be. Be cautious. Don't be resistant to change but examine each new idea carefully. Think about it; review the pros and cons; discuss it with colleagues. Following every new idea will not make you a better teacher. There is not a tick-list of things that you must do to improve. Use each day as a learning experience, evaluating your lessons, looking for the strategies that work. When new ideas head your way, trust your instinct.

The biggest change you will see is that of technology. It will sweep through schools, with glossy brochures promising the world, if only your school buys the latest hardware, IWB, tablet, VLE... You won't recognise all those terms yet, but you will in time. Some technology will prove to be invaluable. The internet is great; VLEs, less so. Smartboards don't revolutionise teaching, but they do provide a medium for visually engaging lessons. Where technology enhances your lessons, use it. If the technology ends up being more important than the learning, then turn it off. Whatever you do, when you hear about Twitter, jump straight in and become an early adopter.

Lessons won't always go the way you had hoped. You will have times when you look around your classroom, questioning your own ability, wondering what happened to make the lesson go so wrong. After all, you planned it well, you even checked it with more experienced colleagues. Don't let it get you down. It happens to everyone, even those colleagues you look up to. Go and talk to them. They may well have some advice that you can use to make it better next time. Tomorrow is a new day and every lesson is a new start. As we tell the children, FAIL is just the First Attempt In Learning.

Teaching is an incredible job. It's so rewarding, but it's never finished. There is always more to do, and it can be easy to push yourself too fast too quickly. Take time to read around education, to research topics that interest you, to develop your own understanding of teaching. Make the most of every opportunity you get and remember: you can do this.

Good luck!

From Andy

Andrew Smith
Assistant principal
Great Heath Academy

Unashamedly love your subject

Dear Jorge,

Congratulations! You've successfully secured a job as a science teacher. You're now responsible for enriching lives and sharing your passion for science. If that sounds scary, it is, and you will have surreal moments when you realise you're on the other side of the room to where you once sat. However, it's the best kind of scary. It's the type of scary where you realise you can actually do something to make someone's life better. I'd like to share three pieces of advice as you embark on the most rewarding journey as a teacher.

First, it must always be about the students. That's why you're there. That's why you do the job you do. You'll encounter people whose priorities perhaps lie elsewhere. You'll most definitely encounter teachers whose priorities are where they should be. Find them. Observe them. Learn everything you can from them. Often the most useful bits of practice you'll see them do are the little unnoticed things: saying hello as they pass a pupil in the corridor, having a quiet word with a student who's not having the best day, and greeting the latecomer with a smile because they know their circumstances and it's a victory just to see them in school! Find those teachers and see how they develop effective pupil relationships. Those relationships are fundamental to effective teaching.

Second, unashamedly love your subject. Students thrive off enthusiasm. Even if they don't yet care for science, they will love to see you get excited about what you teach. Take that enthusiasm and energy and use it to pursue those projects you're passionate about. Make displays, make

Bunsen burner licences and take the time to plan the lesson in a way that hooked them like it did all those years ago. That doesn't mean spending hours tweaking a PowerPoint but rather thinking about how you can explain or demonstrate a concept. Really drill down to the one or two key points of knowledge for that lesson and shape your lesson to be about conveying them effectively and with gusto. Ensure those fundamental concepts are embedded.

Third, don't be afraid to take time for you. The hardest lesson to learn is that you're not superhuman and can't please everyone or do everything. You can say no to tasks. You should also say yes to seeing that friend. Also, get some sleep! Being well rested and happy makes your lessons infinitely better than spending every waking hour fine-tuning everything. The cost of perfection is infinite, so become at ease with imperfection and ensure that you are well yourself.

Teaching is the best job in the world. Live for those eureka moments and revisit them on the tough days.

Good luck!

From Jorge

Jorge Pashler
Science teacher and cadet contingent commander
Westbourne Academy

Welcome home

Dear Emma,

Welcome home.

You're 22 and you're going to love it here. You'll realise that this is truly where you belong. You may feel completely overwhelmed by the fact that you're no longer a student teacher living in Liverpool with your friends, but it's going to be one hell of a new adventure. The fact that the buck now stops with you makes you feel truly sick – and you still haven't even got to grips with the temperamental photocopier or worked out how to use sticky back plastic without sticking yourself, your diary and any other loose or wayward objects together in a gluey mess – but you're really going to love it, I promise.

Your mobile classroom is so dilapidated that it has an actual tree growing up through the store cupboard, the classroom ceiling is propped up by weary jacks and you can only get up the front step sideways because the middle of the step is rotten, but this is your new magical kingdom. There are going to be days when you are completely drowning in paperwork, new information and marking, with a to-do list which extends to multiple pages. There are also going to be days when you laugh so hard that you cry and where children will show you that they are the wisest and kindest people on earth. There will be days when you weep at the injustice and hardship some of them are facing; and there will be days when you weep with pride and awe at their attitudes, their progress and their ability to carry on.

You will get to grips with the acronyms and you'll stop feeling like the biggest imposter ever in staff meetings because your colleagues will teach you and believe in you, just as you do with your pupils. You will thrive on professional learning and you will feel like this is simply what you were meant to do. When your own life is tough – and there are some horrible bumps and unexpected plot twists to come – your classroom will be your sanctuary and where your bruised self-esteem and self-belief will be mended with classroom balm as you realise you are still important, still good at something and still needed. It won't matter what happens in your life, how testing or awful it is; your classroom is where you'll always feel you belong and where, when you close the door, you'll forget about everything and be lost in the joy of being around young people and the privilege of teaching them.

So many people will complain about workload or try to chip away at the positive parts of the job but don't listen to them. You'll become slicker, more efficient and confident as each day passes, and during periods of busyness or pinch points of hard work, you'll become knowing enough to realise that each year has an ebb and flow and that you'll ride each wave more skilfully every time. Your colleagues will become some of your dearest friends, and together you will achieve more and smash systems and outdated approaches in a way you don't think possible right now as your fingers are stuck to the desk with that ruddy sticky back plastic.

So welcome home, Em. This is where you've always belonged, and I'm so glad you found your way here.

From Emma

Emma Turner
Research and CPD lead and author

Without solid foundations, you'll have trouble creating anything of value

Dear Luke,

You had four years of training at university for this career. You built up a wealth of subject knowledge, a plethora of pedagogical styles and a whole host of tools such as AfL and behaviour management. You feel ready and able. What you were not taught, and will continue to learn, is to spend time taking care of the most important part of your most important resource: you.

Looking back, you had a full-on, enjoyable, challenging and progressive NQT year. Teaching was more than you hoped it would be and many of the clichés you see on the teaching recruitment adverts really did happen. The part you were to learn, and perhaps were not supported on so well, was taking care of you, the person. You did not have any worrying levels of stress or anxiety, you did not lose enthusiasm for the job, but you did sacrifice a lot of your time which, had you persisted, may have caused you to burn out. This letter is offering you advice to make sure, when you are ten years into your teaching and your personal life may have more responsibilities (a wife and child), your teaching does not impact on your relationships with them or the other aspects of life you love. This is crucial in ensuring you still remain enthused about your day-to-day teaching, which is why you signed up.

As you train, you will often feel the urge to compare yourself to other teachers. This continues now with social media platforms such as Twitter. Someone is always creating a worksheet, a PowerPoint, a resource that you think, 'Wow, the children must love this' or 'Why didn't I think of this?' A great worksheet or PowerPoint is definitely worthwhile. However, not if you are up until midnight making one. Children respect and learn from strong teachers. A strong teacher is someone who is first and foremost energised, both about their subject and about helping pupils learn. The teacher's personality creates this, not the worksheet or PowerPoint. So whilst you should spend time creating fantastic resources, spend the most time on taking care of you. Have a cut-off point in the evening and certainly over the weekend. Keep up with relationships and hobbies because they shape the best version of you, who in turn then becomes that energised and engaging teacher. Practically, you should spend time finding the best way of managing this for you; however, what works for me now is arriving at school early and leaving at 18.00. I find I can work effectively in that time and therefore take very little, if anything, home. I can then have my evening and my weekend enjoying life away from work, which we all need. Home is home and you feel you have 'finished' work for the day. These timeframes may not work forever and for everyone, but it's important to have boundaries and to stick to these. Technically you never finish in teaching; there is always something you could do. It is therefore vitally important to create boundaries for yourself by creating these cut-off points.

Clear lesson planning routines can also positively impact on your workload. Try not to overcomplicate things. With the support of your mentor, identify clear tangible aims and consider the most straightforward route to get the students there. This will also help to instil good, purposeful routines so that the students know what to expect – and what you expect – when they enter your classroom.

Once you have your classes in good routines, you will find you have a solid foundation to start trying new pedagogical approaches. Remember, without solid foundations in the classroom, you'll have trouble creating anything of value. One of the best tools you will discover is the visualiser. Use this instead of a PowerPoint when modelling; it's a gamechanger and allows you to be responsive to the needs of the students. Mini whiteboards are also a fantastic tool to gather feedback and can be used to compare responses and stimulate rich classroom discussion. Investment your time in deepening your understanding of assessment and feedback and modelling. Done well, it's the staple diet of a great lesson. Observe it in action; watch expert teachers do assessment, feedback and modelling well and ask them about the principles that underpin their approach.

This will never be a 9–3 job, Luke. It can't be. But you must factor in time to make yourself a priority. It's not selfish. It's necessary!

From Luke

Luke Taylor
Physical education and maths teacher
Iceni Academy Methwold